Within
This Wilderness

Other Books by Feenie Ziner

AUTOBIOGRAPHY
A Full House

HISTORICAL NONFICTION
Bluenose, Queen of the Grand Banks
Dark Pilgrim
The Pilgrims & Plymouth Colony

BOOKS FOR CHILDREN
The True Book of Time
Cricket Boy
The Duck of Billingsgate Market
Counting Carnival
The Little Sailor's Big Pet

Within This Wilderness

by Feenie Ziner

A COMMON READER EDITION
THE AKADINE PRESS

Within This Wilderness

A COMMON READER EDITION published 1999
by The Akadine Press, Inc., by arrangement with the author.

A COMMON READER EDITION and fountain colophon are trademarks of The Akadine Press, Inc.

ISBN 1-888173-86-6

10 9 8 7 6 5 4 3 2 1

To Joe

Within
This Wilderness

1

Ben was on perfectly safe ground when he asked me to come out to British Columbia to see where he was living. Any kid who had gone to the trouble of putting a whole continent between himself and his family could count on their never showing up at his doorstep. It wasn't as if we were rich and idle and could hop a plane any time the impulse seized us. No doubt, he didn't actually believe me when I wrote yes, I would spend my three-week vacation with him, squeeze it in between the end of the spring semester and the beginning of summer school. He probably didn't even believe that I had a real job now in a real college, that I wasn't still anchored to the kitchen sink, the eternal mother, tracking my numerous progeny through moody adolescence, reminding them of thank-you notes they had not written, checking their homework, knitting sweaters. It was going on seven years since Ben had flown the nest; a sixteen-year-old fledgling, floundering around on the west coast of Canada. Vancouver was one thing. A city. A recognizable destination. A seven-hour flight from JFK. But the north woods? A six-hour bus trip to the end of the line and after that a bush plane into nowhere? He could not have believed I would really do it.

But I was doing it. I was about to board the bush plane, the earliest passenger to arrive at the terminal. It was housed in a converted Quonset hut at the end of a tatty road. A huge billboard identified it. SEA AND AIR TRANSPORT, it said. YOUR GATEWAY TO ADVENTURE.

Yesterday, when I'd arrived in a taxi from Campbell River with cartons of groceries and baggage, a young woman in the little office—the dispatcher—had persuaded me to stay overnight and take the scheduled flight out at eight in the morning. "A charter would cost you four times as much," she said, "and you wouldn't want to get there in the dark. You might have a long portage at the other end."

Now it was a young man in shirt-sleeves who stood behind the counter. As I opened the glass door, he picked up a pencil and made a crisp check on the flight manifest. He had my name right. There were, I noted, other names on his list.

"You've got twenty minutes," he said.

I fumbled in my wallet with stiff, cold fingers, separating Canadian currency from American. I felt him appraising my new jacket from the L. L. Bean catalogue, taking in the layers of sweaters underneath, the stiff, new blue jeans, the yellow construction boots, and knew myself to look like a cartoon camper in his eyes.

He took my money and paused.

"Aren't you the one called from New York, a couple

of years back?" he asked, smiling with the uncertain superiority of the young. I was glad I had credit with Sea and Air Transport. "Whatever it costs," I'd said, "I'll mail you a check today, if you will just send a plane out and tell him." That was two years ago. The call must have created a sensation.

"Yes," I replied, "that was me."

"There's hot coffee in the machine by the wall," he said, picking up his papers and going into an office behind him. Maybe he was the one. In such a small airline company, the clerks might double as pilots.

If he hadn't smiled in just that way, I might have asked him if he knew Ben, for Ben did come down to Campbell River from time to time—I'd no idea how often—to collect his mail.

"Thanks," I said instead, and reached again into my wallet for a Canadian quarter to plug into the coffee machine. There was a sign above it that said DO NOT USE AMERICAN COINS IN THIS MACHINE.

Alone now in the room, I warmed my hands on the paper cup of coffee and studied a large relief map on the veneer-paneled wall. It was hard to read, for it was covered with a dense grid of numbered squares. I could identify Dyer Strait as the pale blue strip separating the mainland of British Columbia from the Island of Vancouver. I could make out the names of islands in the strait, like Sonora and Quadra—Spanish names, or maybe Indian. But the top of the map was too high to enable me to pick out Proctor's Island from among the blobs of green crowding the northern end of the strait. Overhead, a plane was coming down; underneath the sound of the motor, I thought I heard the young man in the back office asking someone, "Ever hear the one about the tidal wave?" followed by laughter.

"Smart-ass," I thought. "Let them laugh. A young boy, all alone on an island, without a radio or a neighbor or a telephone to tell him that an underwater atom bomb test was about to go off. . . ."

Outside the picture window, a small fleet of fishing boats rocked side by side next to a wharf, their chrome trim gleaming in the clear May sunlight. A cardboard seaplane headed toward them, and stopped at the end of the wharf. It was the plane I was about to board.

The door of the terminal opened, letting in a draft of cold air. A somber-looking man in a worn, leather lumber jacket entered, checked at the counter, and sat down heavily in a vinyl chair. For a moment I thought of taking the seat alongside of him, but he opened a folded newspaper, the *Campbell River Chronicle*, and concealed his face behind it. Then a boy came in, carrying a brace of fishing rods, and, a few moments later, a couple in their twenties and a half-grown dog, black and brown, with immense paws. The dog nearly knocked the young woman over, bounding past her, and dashed about the waiting room, jumping on and off chairs, licking his master's face, the clerk's face, the face of the man behind the newspaper. I wanted to catch the young woman's eye, desperate, suddenly, to tell someone where I was going, to leave behind some trace of my passage. But she took a seat as far as possible from the man who was reading and stared at the floor in a closely-guarded reverie. Her young man pursued the dog around the room, wrestled it onto the scale. The pointer swung wildly.

"Seventy-five pounds," I heard the clerk say. And when he told the young man how much it would cost to take the dog on the plane, my mental calculator flipped. No one had remembered to weigh my parcels. Through the picture window, I could see a man wheeling a hand truck toward the end of the wharf, and I recognized the load. Suitcases and grocery cartons, with a bunch of celery sticking out of the top. I hurried outside and said, "I don't think I have enough money to pay for that, if you charge for cargo by the pound."

"You the one looking for her son?" he asked.

I nodded.

"Get in," he said, and handed me up a thin, wobbly ladder into the cabin of the plane. I clutched my briefcase with Ben's letter inside, confirming the date of my arrival. I was a day late, for I hadn't counted on spending a night in Campbell River, hadn't thought the grocery shopping would take so long. "Just bring fresh food," Ben had written. "I've got staples." My three-week supply of groceries took up all the cargo space behind the seats.

I took the one nearest the cabin door and drew my watch out from under the layered sweaters. It was an antique, an heirloom. I wore it on a chain around my neck. Opening the thin silver case with a fingernail, I thought how dumb of me to expose that delicate mechanism to God knows what. But I'd put it on at the last minute, thinking that if I were crushed, drowned, maimed, or rendered unconscious, whoever came upon my remains would find it, read my name engraved on the silver in a flowing script, ponder the hairline Roman numerals, and say, "Behold, she was really somebody."

"Promise me you won't do anything rash," my eldest son had said the day I left home.

I looked at the watch for a long time before the position of the hands said, "two minutes past eight." The other passengers were all in their places, staring straight ahead as if we were on a subway. The dog, too, had preceded me. He tried to climb out of the open door, but was stopped by the ladder. His master grabbed him by the scruff of the neck and pushed him onto the floor, but the dog escaped again, put a heavy paw on my lap, licked my face, then turned round and round in the aisle, whimpering and drooling.

My nylon sleeping bag was the last thing on the hand truck, and the man on the wharf tossed it on top of the groceries, bending the celery. He slammed the plane door shut and the pilot climbed into his seat, unsmiling. A fine-boned man in shirt-sleeves. Not the sort of man I could work my way up the aisle to ask: "You're sure you know where we're going?" Maybe he was the one who'd said to Ben, "You're coming with me to Campbell River, kid—your mother wants you on the phone." He leaned far to the right and cranked up a wheel on the floor of the cockpit, the way men in the silent movies of my childhood used to crank up cars, except that, when the motor started, he did not run around the outside of the plane and jump into his seat, the way they used to. As the motor wound to a roar, the dog, whimpering, panting, and swallowing his spittle, crouched beside his master. The fragile craft shuddered. Sick with fright, the brown and black puppy hurled himself against the cabin door. We ripped across the wind-ruffled surface of the lagoon. I held the craft together with the tendons of my neck. As we lifted clear of the water, the plane tilted sharply against the tongue of land that marked the edge of the town. Every hair on the dog's body stood erect. His master reached out a hand and said, "Down, Java!" but his mistress stared stonily ahead, as if words cost money.

In the distance, the jagged snow peaks of the Cascade Coastal Range reached like a stiff, white meringue toward a pink horizon. The islands crowding Dyer Strait were great, green knobs of land rising steeply out of the sea, a hundred miles north of Vancouver and a hundred miles south of the Queen Charlotte Islands. No gentle slopes footed them out. There were no beaches, no docks, no human structures. Save for the veined declivities where waterfalls or river beds eroded the rock and the paler green of hardwoods contoured the land, the islands were blanketed with black green forest. We rode the air currents flowing over and around them. Directly below, fishing boats the size of matches left Vs of white froth on the watered silk of the strait. We were flying over the last and final untamed wilderness in North America.

It clouded up and began to rain; the summits of islands were veiled in mist. Leaning against my window, I watched an eagle circling below, watched as we dropped alongside it and then below it, making our first descent, smooth as a goose going down for a foot-first landing on the water. In a few moments the cabin door opened. I could see a rough-hewn wharf with a big mailbox on the end of it, and a sign that said ICE. On a piece of land gouged out of a hillside stood a log cabin—not a store, but a fishing station. A red-faced man in high rubber boots took a package from the pilot and handed him another, and the boy with the fishing rods got out. He stepped over a raft of loose open boats to reach the pier. Someone outside said "day guide," but the expression on the boy's face did not suggest an outing.

The door slammed, the plane taxied out to open water and climbed once more toward the clouds. At the next stop, the man in the lumber jacket got off. Not a word was exchanged. Had they all forgotten how to talk?

The couple with the dog got off at the next stop. "You're last," the pilot said, glancing briefly over his shoulder without making eye contact with me. But before the door shut, a tall, lanky man hurried, limping, toward the plane, carrying a pair of knee-high boots caked with mud. He dropped them alongside my groceries and pulled himself in after them. Holding one leg stiffly in the aisle, he let himself down painfully into the seat in front of mine, half-turned, and said with a sigh, "Goin' in to Campbell River to have this bum knee looked after." He was gaunt and needed a shave, but his back was straight as a plumb line.

"How did you hurt it?" I shouted over the noise of the plane.

He looked startled, then pulled his pant leg up to expose a swollen, purple contusion. "Hit by a loose buckle, five days ago."

Somewhere in the suitcase behind me was a first-aid kit, sent to me by my doctor-brother all the way from Texas. "Never mind, you'll need them!" he'd insisted. A dozen vials labeled for mild pain, for severe pain, for diarrhea, for insomnia, for nausea, for acute infection, for fever. Ace bandages and splints, sterile gauze, disinfectants, adhesive tape. Nothing in the kit for being out of one's mind, nothing for vertigo from peering over the rim of the known world.

"Good thing you're taking care of it. A knee can be a lot of trouble."

He pushed his woolen cap down over his eyebrows and back up again. His eyes were intensely blue and depthless, as if his character were imprinted entirely from the outside. "Got a couple of days coming. Thought I'd see the doctor. Can't afford to lose the power in my legs," he added knowingly. He eyeballed my groceries, scrutinized me critically. I looked down at my yellow boots that still smelled of the Army-Navy store.

"Goin' to see my son," I said in a clumsy effort to alter my New York accent.

"He live up here?" The eyebrows disappeared under his cap.

"Uh-huh. . . ."

"He a logger?"

"Well, sort of . . ."

We reached altitude and I checked my watch again. The tip of the wing inched across a broad band of shaven hillside—a gash of dark clay, red as caked blood, as even-edged and arbitrary as if a razor had slashed the mountain's green beard. Stripped logs cascaded down the hillside like a spill of toothpicks. I tapped the logger on the shoulder.

"Is *that* how they cut timber?"

"Oh, don't worry, lady," he said, rubbing his nose with the back of a brown, gnarled hand, "it grows right back."

"But there's nothing left!"

He pulled himself quite around in his seat and said patiently, "Trees got spirit. The part you cut is only the *outward manifestation* of the spirit. It's not the real tree." He paused, nodded abruptly, and added "Yessir! Even the Indians know that!" I lost the rest of his theology in the engine's noise, for we were peeling down toward a lake in the middle of an island. Rain poured down the window glass, and all outdoors was a blur of wet. We sailed over another slashed hillside, then down, down, rushing past out-of-focus forest until the plane struck the rain-pocked surface of the lake. We skidded a short way and stopped, floating in the stillness of the middle of nowhere. No sign of a float, of a cabin, of a trail of smoke. Not even a beach. Through the window on my side, I made out a dense curtain of evergreens lining the shore, their lower branches trailing in the water. On the other side, a palisade of silver gray snags, gaunt as gallows, formed a barrier between the water and the living wood.

The pilot leaned forward, peering through the windshield. "Well," he observed with his hands on his knees, "this is Tibbett Lake." Clearly, he was waiting for me to get out.

"But my son isn't here!"

"That's not *my* fault, lady," he replied, and glanced at his wristwatch. "We're already 'way behind schedule."

I climbed toward the cockpit. Although I knew the question was impertinent, I asked, "Do you have a map?"

Irritably, he pulled a post-card-sized map from a clip of papers tucked above the windshield and pointed to a patch of blue as big as a pencil point.

"Where are we? I mean, at which end of the lake?"

"West. But there's nothing at all at the other end."

"There's not very much here, either," I said, and he glared at me—". . . goddamn hippie, draft dodger, hiding out," written all over his face.

The logger hobbled, stooping, toward the cockpit.

"Go on, Mac," he said, cajoling, "give the other end a try."

The pilot compressed his lips and gunned the motor. We scudded down the lake, passing one tiny island after another. What if Ben wasn't here? I had no alternative plan, nothing in reserve, no expedients at my disposal. I was four thousand miles from home and the only person I knew in British Columbia was Ben. There was no retreat, no midpoint to which I could return to await further word. Either he turned up in the next few seconds or I headed straight back to where I had come from and gave up on him, forever. Could it be that in a last-minute panic, he had decided that he did not want to see me after all? Or was he lying somewhere in that wet jungle with a broken back, or a bullet wound, or worse?

Then, through the streams of water running down my window, I saw a yellow dot.

"Is that someone?" I shouted. The pilot squinted, pulled the stick toward himself, and took the plane toward the yellow dot until it became the figure of a man standing on the water. As we drew closer, I could see that he was standing on the end of a huge, partially submerged log. His hands were thrust deep into the pockets of a bright yellow rain jacket, as if he were very cold. The plane moved slowly, bumping gently across the water.

Suddenly, the still figure sprang into motion, running the length of the log back toward the shore. With a great leap from the end of the fallen tree, he disappeared into the forest.

"What the hell!" the logger murmured, behind me.

It was Ben, all right. I'd know that gallop anywhere. He was fleeing my arrival, telling me to turn back, to go away, to leave him alone. What was I to do? Chase him through the woods, calling "Ben! Ben! Don't be afraid—it's me! It's only your mother!"

And then, he burst through the foliage carrying a coil of rope. Gaining the top of the log in a single stride, he leaned over the water and tossed an end of the rope to the pilot, who by now had climbed out onto the plane's wing. Each of them shortened the rope until the plane was close enough to the log for the pilot to straddle it. Securing the craft, the pilot began unloading, handing one grocery carton after another to Ben, who carried them on his shoulder to the shore. Lightened, the plane rose perceptibly on the water.

"You'll never make it in them shoes," the logger said to me, critically. "Better use mine. They're caulk-soled." He watched solicitously as I exchanged my boots for his. I tied my boots together by the laces and slung them over my shoulder, to leave my arms free for balancing.

"That's right!" he called after me from the door of the plane, "Don't be scared. You'll make it!"

Step after step, I placed one wobbly foot in front of the other until I reached the end of the log. It was a far jump from its rounded, weathered surface to the sandy little beach, but I took it without hesitating, dropping briefly to my knees as I hit the sand, and saying, "That pilot!" as I dusted off the bulging knees of my blue jeans.

I changed back into my own boots and, with decorum, passed the logger's boots to Ben, who passed them to the pilot. I waved the logger my gratitude and the logger waved back. The pilot climbed in and shut the door; the propeller whirled and the big cardboard goose turned tail, waddling out toward the center of the lake.

I took a deep breath, ready to holler, "Hey! Wait!" For suddenly, I wanted to escape the austere young man who strode the log's length toward me. "Hey!" I wanted to shout to the pilot, "You won't forget to come back? To rescue me?"

Enfolded in a blinding embrace, Ben's black beard brushed against my cheek, and for one split second in the earth's long turning, I was home, free.

2

It was nearly two years since he'd been home. He'd grown,
or so it seemed to me, for I did not remember reaching up
so far to touch his face. His wild, black hair was trimmed
to the bottom of his ears. His still-scant beard was black,
short, and neatly combed. He was thicker in the chest. The
flannel shirt underneath the rain jacket hung loosely; rum-
pled, but clean. He wore a ragged tuque set squarely on his
brow, like the logger on the plane.

Side by side on the tiny strand we watched the plane
as it diminished, then rose with a shrill whine up into the
sky to disappear under the cover of cloud. My baggage
stood on the sand, in the lee of a single-seated kayak. An
elegant craft, shapely as a willow leaf, with an open eye
painted on the prow—gazing, as if hypnotized, upon
stones.

"You built that yourself, Ben?"

14

"Last year."

He hoisted a box of groceries lightly to his shoulder, grasped my heavy suitcase with his free hand, and gestured with his head for me to follow. "I'll come back in a minute to get the rest," he said. His voice was rusty.

But he walked like the lord of the land, rubber boots clumping carelessly against the wet earth. Leading the way, he took a path hidden from the lake by a lush growth of alder, freshly leaved, gleaming with raindrops, magnifying the light. The ground was brown and springy, thickly matted with forest fallings, disintegrating timber, patches of long grass, bent, heavy with rain. My focus blurred. I was swimming downward, following a beam of deflected light, dropping lower and lower until my fingers grazed a jagged reef. I moved in slow motion, lungs straining against the pressure of depth until a piercing cry hauled me abruptly to the surface. It was a bird call. Sharp, reportorial, devoid of sentiment. Fumbling in my pocket for a handkerchief I asked myself, "What is there to cry about now? You've found him, haven't you?"

The path opened into a dome-shaped clearing. Dim, vast, curtained by walls of evergreen. Tier upon tier of fir, balsam, hemlock and cedar whose trunks converged a mile or so overhead. A vertical, pillared space, solemn as a cathedral. Bells, deep-throated bells, should be bong-bonging, monks reading their breviaries to the sound of chants. But there was only the thin harping of the wind and the harsh conversation of one winged creature with another.

Ben turned back to measure his triumph by my awe.

"I tried to tell you. . . ." he said, and I knew he wanted to believe that my tears were only for the trees.

A strange little structure stood in the center of the

clearing, something between a geodesic dome and an A-frame, partially covered with plastic sheeting, and sheathed to the waist with cedar shingles. A bay bulged from one side, and the odor of burning wood and fresh coffee made the glands of my jawbone ache.

On either side of the little house, workbenches winged out, each of them knee-deep in cedar shavings. The one on my right lay open to the weather, was laden with freshly planed logs. The other, closer to the house, had a high tent of clear plastic fastened to the trees overhead, just enough shelter to keep off the rain. Under it, Ben had his sleeping space, a rumple of familiar-looking blankets piled on half of a large platform. On the other half lay a litter of mallets, chisels, saws and hammers, as if work were his bedmate. He apologized for his unmade bed. "Just woke up when I heard the plane," he said, but, before I inquired if he still made a habit of sleeping late, he interjected justification: "I didn't get to sleep until dawn. Man, what a clean-up!"

With a deft movement of his boot, he kicked open the weighted flap at the rear end of the little house and ushered me in. "The delivery entrance," he said. "You don't mind?"

The interior was a dozen feet in length and half as wide. It was warm and dry inside, and neater than any space I had ever known him to occupy. Pots and skillets lined the wall at the near end, clothing hung from a row of pegs. A great plank, the split half of a tree, lined the length of the house and opposite it a big cast-iron stove, which Ben called the Airtight, stood on iron feet on the dirt floor, its chimney braces festooned with drying socks. A coffee pot hissed and steamed on the flat, iron top.

"You could make the centerfold of *House Beautiful,* Ben!" I said.

He set the first box of groceries on the bench.

"I haven't tasted fresh food for months, except for the deer I shot ten days ago."

"With a bow and arrow?"

"With a rifle," he replied, glancing obliquely at my face to see if I was joking. I was not.

While he went back to the beach to bring in the rest of my gear, I poured a cup of coffee into a thick, chipped mug, wrapped my hands around its warmth, and looked over his bookshelf. The marker in the *William Faulkner Treasury* I'd sent him was close to the end. Good. The cover of the *I Ching* showed the most wear. Bad. There were books on house construction, boat building, and a field guide to mushrooms. There were Nietzsche, Tolkien, Vonnegut, and Velikovsky. Still long on fantasy, short on facts. There was the *Thurber Carnival* I gave him. So he laughed, too, once in a while. I wondered what he would make of the two-volume Proust I'd brought him, he being the only person in North America who had enough time to read it.

It seemed much lighter inside the house than outdoors. Perhaps it was the intelligence, the order, the caring about my opinion that I saw in the rows of jars and tin cans at the end of the long bench, each of them sorted, purposeful: smoker's things, scissors and cutting tools, sewing articles, toiletries.

The alcove behind the Airtight was a little pantry, arched at the entrance, with its walls curved outward something like the entrance to an igloo. Handmade boxes of cedar, each with a carefully fitted lid, lined the wall, no two alike. There were large tins and covered glass jars, and a propane camp stove standing on a box. There was only one chair, massive and well-made, with foamrubber stitched across the back and a carpet sample to warm and soften the seat. It stood close to the stove, a meager concession to physical comfort, and utterly solitary.

It was amazing how the house was put together. Its joints were held together by string, wood lashed to wood and tightly wound. Not a single ninety-degree angle in the whole structure.

Ben did not bring the smell of the outdoors indoors, as he lined up the four grocery boxes on the shelf-bench, because the smell of outdoors was already indoors. But the house expanded in his presence, was filled with the odor of plenty. He exclaimed over the provisions, astounded by the wisdom, the shrewdness, the economy, the farsightedness of my shopping; I, with my quarter-century in supermarkets. Apples, oranges, potatoes, onions, carrots, cabbage, the bent celery, each plastic bagful a miracle, to him, of transportation, distribution, wholesaling and retailing, to say nothing of fertilization, unionization, profit and loss.

"These will keep in the shed," he decided, sorting. The shelves of the shed near his bed were open, I recalled. "Won't some animal pinch them out there?"

He shook his head, no.

"Don't tell me that the bears on Proctor's Island are more respectful of private property than the suburban raccoons back home," I said, hoping he'd scoff and say, "There are no bears on Proctor's Island." But instead he said, "They won't smell it through the plastic."

Item by item, he exclaimed over the luxury of canned hams, over five pounds of raisins, a big bottle of white wine, and a small one of cognac, a gift from his older brother. *Cookies!* Three for the road, crammed one after the other into his mouth, and the rest popped into a tightly lidded metal container in the pantry.

"The perishables go into my refrigerator," he said. This was a cedar cabinet with a leather-hinged door. It opened in the same direction as the one back home, but this door was delicately curved at the top, rather in the outline of a mosque, as if to say that what lay inside was sacred. It had a strong gamey smell—a haunch of venison. There was nothing else. I tucked a big Polish sausage around it and asked, "Will they fight?"

Ben wanted me to admire the thin strip of foam rubber tacked around the edges of the door: "mouse-proofing." And the craftily screened hole at the back that opened to the fresh air and kept things cool. He put the butter inside, the three small rounds of hard cheese, and kept the cottage cheese on the wooden shelf, consuming half of it as we unpacked. I tried not to wonder what he would have eaten this day, if I had not done the marketing.

"Fresh fruit!" he cried, biting noisily into an apple. "You know, Mom, since I've been up here I've learned how to eat with my mouth open?"

"You stayed at the new motel in Campbell River last night? I thought you'd be here yesterday."

"No, Ben, it was much too fancy for me. I did walk over there when I got off the bus from Vancouver, but all those BankAmericard businessmen with matching luggage, peeling out of taxis, headed for the bar, intimidated me. I knew I had this big marketing to do before I took the bush plane. I just couldn't see myself going into a place like that—they probably have a kidney-shaped, heated swimming pool and all that—with a load of groceries. I've got standards."

"I know," he said.

"I thought I'd get a plane out right away, so I took all my truck out to the airport in a cab. We passed the Indian reservation on the point. Hovels. Christ, that strip looks just like Central Avenue. "Gateway to the Sportsman's Paradise" on every other sign. It was nearly sunset by that time, and I was pretty beat after six hours on the bus up from Vancouver. Talk about the end of the world! The woman at Sea and Air Transport told me to wait until this morning, that a charter would cost a mint. So I asked the cab driver to take me to an inexpensive place to spend the night. He was very obliging. I stayed at a place called the Carioca Motel, with neon palm trees on the sign."

"Haw! Haw!" Ben said, chuckling into his beard, "Campbell River's red-light district!"

"Well, sin isn't all it's cracked up to be. I was never so cold in my life. The damned dial on the space heater came off in my hand when I tried to warm the place up. It was just about the saddest room I've ever slept in. I kept getting up all through the night, watching for the morning. . . . You know, Sea and Air Transport didn't even charge me by weight for the groceries?"

He frowned at the mention of money. He always frowned when I talked about money.

"That damned pilot," I went on, reaching back for common ground, "wanted to drop me off at the other end of the lake. I wouldn't have found you in a million years. Say, was he the same guy who . . .?"

"No, it was another one. Listen, Mom, I'm not sore about that call any more."

"I hoped you weren't, Ben. I had no intention of humiliating you, of making you look like a fool in their eyes. It's just so hard to explain things at this distance. When you told me over the phone that your island was circled by mountains, I was astounded. I thought of an island like Nantucket. Flat and sandy."

("Do you think everybody out here is an *idiot?*" he'd demanded of me.)

"I tried to write you about it, but there was no way a letter could convey that particular atmosphere, that sense of crisis. Every hour the radio and the TV announcers were reporting warnings from scientists, protests. I'd already sent four letters to Congress, and a telegram to the Supreme Court—it went all the way up to the United States Supreme Court, Ben . . ." I could see one of my own speeches on the nature of public responsibility for the democratic process encapsulating in his mind, and went on. "They were saying that California might crack at the San Andreas fault and slide into the sea from the shock. And then they started talking about the possibility of a tidal wave. All I could think of was a wall of water with a thousand miles of Pacific power behind it, piling into Dyer Strait. I pictured you standing on the shore, looking out to sea, not knowing what was coming. And I didn't ask them to bring you to Campbell River, or to phone me. All I asked was for someone to try to find you, to warn you. God, Ben, anything could have happened, and we wouldn't even have known if you were dead or alive. . . . The second I heard your voice I knew you were mad, that to you it was just like the time I called the principal at Springhurst Primary to ask him to tell you to be sure to wear your galoshes home because it was raining . . ."

"It sure as hell was," he said. "But I told you. I got over it. I was only mad for the moment . . ."

"I guess I'm a legend in my own time down at Sea and Air. The guy at the counter knew who I was the minute I opened the door. He didn't even ask me my name. By the way, Ben, how do I get out of here three weeks from now? I didn't make a reservation because I didn't know how long I'd be staying."

"You'll stay until the meeting, I hope."

"There's a meeting? With who?"

"With the Company—the guys who run this place. I'm sort of counting on your being there. You'll give our side class."

Before I could ask more about the meeting, he added "The plane flies over every day. You take a boat out to the middle of the lake and flag them down with a blanket."

"Suppose they're looking the other way?"

"You do it over again the next day," he replied, grinning. "Don't worry, we'll manage something." And patted me paternally on the head.

We opened the suitcase after lunch. Every member of the family had sent something along for Ben. Clothing, a drawing and a poem, a sealed envelope from his older brother Jesse, which, I suspected, contained money. "How is everybody?" he asked me softly, visibly touched by these emblems of remembrance. To his younger siblings, Ben was a hero, a figure of mystery and high adventure. To his father and to me . . .

"Adam's something of an overachiever at the moment. President of the junior class, captain of the wrestling team, lead in the school play. Ricky's fine. Crazy about cars. He felt bad at not sending anything, but he said to give you his love and tell you he'll be out here next, as soon as he graduates."

"Good ole Ricky!"

"Janet still reads two books a day, draws a lot. Something of a loner, like Dad. Jesse and Meg are both working —doing well."

"And Dad?"

"He's really into sculpture now. Working in stainless steel. He would pick the hardest medium there is. You know Dad. An iron will."

Each of us had our private vision of Hal, the father, husband, artist, bent hour after hour over his work, all domestic and commercial endeavor being, to him, a digression from his true purpose.

"Would he ever come out here, do you think? What he could do with all this wood! Did you ever see such wood?"

I did not want to say, now, that a shortage of raw materials was the least of his father's worries. Time was what Hal never had enough of. Four years ago, I had prevailed upon him to make the trip to Vancouver to see what Ben was doing with his life. Ben was living in the attic of a dilapidated garage and attending an art school when the spirit moved him. He'd already been on the west coast for two years, had made a few trips back home on money we'd sent him. He was vague about his life. His speech was full of terms like "cosmic energy" and "inner space." It was Haight-Ashbury time in American life, and in the moments when I was capable of positive thinking I consoled myself that it was a fashionable trend he was living out, that it was a passing phase in his youth. "There's nothing wrong with him," Hal would say. "He just hates regimentation. So do I. He'll find himself eventually, if you just give him enough time. Stop torturing yourself."

Who can understand how a man thinks about a son? True, my husband had lived in the wilderness of British

Columbia for two years himself, most of the time in isolation, but it was forced upon him. He was in the Army
Engineers when the Alcan Highway was being built.

"But you'd never have done it out of choice," I said.
Which, he acknowledged, was true.

It was a large effort for him to leave his job, to fly to
Vancouver; and, though he tried to paint a cheerful picture
for me, I read a different message from his report. I wasn't
happy about Ben's friends, a subdued and secretive lot who
sat around reading and listening to an expensive hi-fi, who
regarded Ben's father as a spy. "Ben lives upstairs," Hal
said, "I think because downstairs is such a mess. There was
cat fur in the stew, paw prints on the butter. When I
walked in, a goddamned monkey jumped on my shoulder
and peed right down my collar. Goddamned animals had
more energy than the kids." But Ben, he claimed, was glad
to see him and had painted the ends of all the loose floor-
boards white, lest they rise up and smite his father on the
head if he stepped upon them.

"And what is he doing with his time?"

"Lots of painting."

"Any good?"

"Terrific, as a matter of fact. All he needs is instruc-
tion. He's got plenty of talent."

"And how is he supporting himself?"

"Odd jobs."

"Does he have enough to live on?"

"I guess so. The way he lives."

No, Hal was not likely to make another trip. Overpro-
tectiveness was not his style.

I reached into the suitcase and unwrapped a package.
"Dad sent you these," I said, avoiding an answer to Ben's
question.

The package contained a set of Japanese brushes, cakes of sumi ink, and a fine, blank sketchbook. Taking it from my hands and opening it, a stillness fell over Ben, a heavy-lidded quiet like the perfect roundness of a full moon on the unbroken surface of a pond. He sank into himself, out of my sight. Where was he going? Whose song did he hear? I watched him fingering the brushes, twirling each one into a point against his palm. He looked like an old baby, with his high, rounded brow serene as Buddha's.

"Ninety percent of my wealth comes from home," he said at last. And reached for the new woolen cap his older brother had sent him. As he put it on, I noticed that among the coal black strands of his hair there were now a few threads of silver.

3

I would have thought that Ben would leave the drawing supplies out on the bench where he could get to them as soon as we settled into a routine, but instead he drew a battered old suitcase out from under the bench and opened it on the floor. "My treasure chest," he said. On top of the folded clothing was a ragged sketchbook, the edges of the pages gray with usage.

"Could I see that?" I asked.

"There's nothing worthwhile in it," he said. "Just some sketches, designs, notes I've written to myself when I had no one else to talk to."

Placing his father's gifts beside it, he snapped the lock shut and put the suitcase back under the shelf.

"I've got a present for you, too," he said, reaching for a small box on a high shelf. "I bought these the last time I had some cash."

"How nice!" Full of expectation, I opened his gift with care.

"Bullets! For me?"

"They aren't bullets, Mom, they're flares."

"Oh."

"Visible for fifty miles. Three seconds each. So you can stop worrying about me."

"Thanks. Thanks, heaps. But is anyone around, for fifty miles?"

"Of course. Plenty of people."

"Is Gilly back?" I knew Gilly, knew her very well, had held her in my arms a year ago when she had come east, while she wept over her failure to hit it off with Ben. "Forget him, Gilly dear," I'd urged her. "You've got to make a life of your own. You can't hang around and let yourself get hurt."

She was such a vulnerable girl, holding Ben up as some kind of demigod, a ground-breaker who defied the elements, defied society, defied the Establishment in order to blaze new trails to spiritual purity. I wished they could have made it together, too; selfishly, because, if Gilly lived with him, he would not be living alone. But I could see that she was becoming as estranged from the world as he, and tried to persuade her to take another course. Some months later, Ben wrote that she'd married a young fellow who lived on Proctor's Island, summers. "Just a formality," he'd written, adding that she'd taken out the marriage license between going to Sears and the Motor Vehicles Bureau in Campbell River. "She needed to be married to a Canadian, for immigration purposes," he had explained.

Now Ben said, "Yes, Gilly and Ellis came back a few

weeks ago. They're over on Forsook Lake. She'll be glad to
see you, Mom."

"Is she happy with her husband?"

He shrugged. "I guess so. Yeah, I guess she's all right."

"She told you she'd come to see me?"

"Uh-hum. She stayed east after that for quite a while.
Got a job as a housepainter, then as a dogcatcher. Then she
lived in Vermont for awhile. But she likes it out west better."

He looked uncomfortable, and changed the subject.
"Diana and Dale and the kids are here, too. You'll like Dale
Finn. He's a fantastic person."

I hated Dale Finn. I'd never met him, but Ben's letters
always mentioned Dale. He was an older man with a family, and I guessed he was some kind of a guru to Ben, some
kind of an over-age hippie with a lot of mystifying, meta-
physical talk, a Robin Hood who needed Ben to play Little
John. "And who else, besides them?"

"Buddhi just came back. He lives on one of those islands you passed coming in on the plane."

"Would you say there were ten people in a hundred
square miles?"

"You make it sound awful. It only takes a couple of
hours to get to another person, now that it's spring."

He needed a little coaxing before he would tell me how
he happened to choose this particular place for a campsite,
since the Finns lived on the shore of a lake called Capaswap, even farther away than Gilly's.

"Dale and I were on a hunting trip together, the first
time I saw it," he said. "I'd been living over on another
island until then, but, well . . . there was some trouble. The

Forestry Service burned my house down. It wasn't much of a house, just an old generator shack, but they didn't like the idea of anyone living in it. I was looking for another place. We were paddling down Tibbett Lake when I saw this tall snag up on the mountain, and it spelled my name. 'Ben's,' it said."

"So? Go on . . ."

"So a couple of weeks later, I decided to move here. I was coming across the lake in the kayak and it began to snow. It was November, two-and-a-half years ago. Big, heavy flakes. I had a roll of plastic, string, rice, matches, a hatchet, and a metal pot up in the forward end of the kayak."

"That's all you brought?"

"That's all I needed. Plastic is a great material. Plastic is to us what horses were to the Spanish."

I could see him censoring his story, fidgeting with a pipe, tamping down the tobacco, and taking a long time putting matches to it.

"I pulled up on the beach, put up my plastic tent, built a good fire, cooked up the rice. There's terrifically good water in the stream alongside here. By that time it was snowing like a sonofabitch."

A stick of wood crackled like gunshot in the Airtight and I shifted in the big chair.

". . . and then I sat down under the tent to dry out and eat. Had a real good place fixed up in there. Then I heard something. A footstep."

"Friday's?"

"No, a wolf. She was sitting on the other side of my fire, looking me over."

"So what did you do?"

"Just what you taught me: I said politely, "Good evening, Mrs. Wolf."

"And what did she say?"

"She didn't say anything because just at that moment the snow on top of the tent got so heavy the whole thing collapsed on my head. Was I sore! When I climbed out, I caught a glimpse of her hightailing it around the lake. Laughing her head off."

"Wolves laugh?"

"Of course. Wolves have a great sense of humor."

"Are there many wolves on Proctor's Island?"

"Not too many. Most of them live up on the mountain behind us. Usually, when I meet them in the woods, they run away. Why, you aren't scared, are you?"

"Of course not. You don't think I'd have come all the way up here without having done my homework, do you? I've read Farley Mowat. Why, wolves are practically man's best friends!"

So we lied to one another. I wondered what the true story of Ben's coming here was, and if he would ever tell it to me.

Before we left the little house, Ben showed me how to dispose of the dishwater. You kicked open the flap of the back door and, grasping the dishpan with both hands, heaved it outside in as wide an arc as you could without throwing yourself after it. In this way, he explained, the detergents would not pollute Cryptic Creek, which ran a few yards from his house.

"Come on, I'll show you the water supply," he said, and crossed a little rise.

A small shelf of rock extended over a pool; in its shadow hung inch-long fingerlings of trout and salmon, which darted out of sight as Ben knelt on a fallen log, a bridge vine-wound and worn flat by usage. An enormous tangle of fallen timber lay just above the crossing point, the legacy of the wasteful men who had felled the ancestors of the present forest, about seventy-five years ago. Ben had cleared some of the dead timber away to make room for salmon to swim upriver to spawn. Where the water slipped under the old wood, a little falls murmured sociably, filling the somber space with chatter. Ben pointed out a knee-high hemlock he'd transplanted beside the stream. "It stood in the way of the house," he said, regarding it with affection. "It's doing real well over here."

"Now I'll show you the shitter," he said, climbing the slope beyond the creek. It was much steeper on this side, wilder and craggier than the woods around the house. I took two steps for every one of his. We climbed so far up that I could barely make out the shed and the workbenches below. The facility was a wooden platform built out from a huge stump, about twenty feet in girth. Enclosed by boards on the side facing the house, the platform was reached by climbing over the protruding roots of the stump. There was nothing to hold on to, on top. On the first and broadest of the three planks of the platform stood a covered plastic bucket filled with wood ash; in it lay a small red shovel. On the bucket's exterior, in elegant gothic lettering, it said FLUSH. The other two boards were separated from one another by a foot-wide space: the business section. "You just sprinkle a thin layer of wood ash around afterward," Ben said. And I knew that whatever other thoughts might weigh on my mind, as long as I were here the use of the facility would be first on my list of traumatic preoccupations.

I had assumed that I would sleep in the little house; on

the bench, perhaps, or on a bed of balsam boughs piled on the dirt floor. But Ben said he'd fixed up a real bed for me in a place he called the Kiosk. While I zipped myself back into my rain jacket, he lectured me on the importance of keeping my feet dry, no matter what. Whatever else happened, I must not catch cold. Rain, he said, comes and goes all year 'round, not just in the month of May. Dry socks were the *sine qua non* of Proctor's Island living. The only certain method for drying socks was to hang them beside the Airtight.

Beyond the campsite, the land sloped sharply upward, part of the same slope the facility was built on but on the opposite side of Ben's house. Here the trees were the thickness of telephone poles and had nearly as little foliage down below. Their leafing did not begin until after the first hundred feet. There were few vines, no parasitic growths, almost no underbrush; just a sprinkling of tiny orange mushrooms, like exclamation points on a background of moss and low fern. It was a healthy, well-spaced woods, sober and tranquil, with an easy wind song in the trees. I could hear the lake at the base of the slope but could not see it, for the trees below were draped to the foot, forming a dense screen, like a scrim. Up ahead stood another little structure, bowed-out like the house but more in the shape of a wind sock, with a large, triangular opening facing the lake. Plastic was secured to a wooden frame of cedar and tied in a bunch at the uphill end. No shingles obstructed the view through the plastic sheeting. Inside, I felt as though I were in a fishbowl.

There was a sturdy wooden bed with a curved headboard, just such a bed as the dwarfs might have offered Snow White. A double layer of foam rubber and a handmade pillow stuffed with balsam were laid on it. The bed was flanked on one side by a neatly lidded cedar chest containing Ben's dress clothes, and on the other by an inverted oil drum which served as a night table.

"It's darling," I said with a comma in my voice. "You mean I'm going to sleep in here all alone? Couldn't you stay here, too? I mean, couldn't we be broad-minded?"

"No," he replied, "You'll be fine in here." And admired my new sleeping bag.

"Guaranteed for twenty below zero, it said in the Bean catalogue."

"Oh, you'll be plenty warm enough."

I knew he was disappointed that I did not exclaim over the accommodation. I could see what pains he'd taken to provide me with the very best he had. But the words refused to come. "One thing at a time," I told myself, and followed him back to the house.

We spent the rest of the afternoon in talk. I tried to tell him about my job, but it had no reality to him that, in the years of his absence, I had become a college professor. It had little enough reality for me either, now that I was here. Moreover, it was a risky topic; for, if I made my small successes too important, he might interpret my message as "See? I've made it inside the system. Why can't you?" I did not wish to hear another denunciation from him of the hypocrisy and irrelevance of formal education, to hear it described once more as an empty symbol of middle-class status. He did not want to hear about people he had never met, he wanted details about the people he knew, people who cared about him. He took in family gossip like a dry sponge, affirming with a nod, a grin, a frown how exquisitely present we all were in his mind, every quirk and foible apprehended and embraced.

When I'd exhausted family news, I took a flyer in the direction of the *I Ching*, let it drop that I was "into" a bit of the old Tao myself.

"You never used to be interested in all that stuff," he said.

"I've learned a thing or two since you left," I replied. And told him about the commentaries I'd read on the Book of Changes, how the ancient Chinese had no conception of progress, how I thought the yin and the yang had their correspondence in Jung's concept of the anima and the animus.

He was astounded that a serious literature on the subject existed in English. "You're the first person I've met who's really trying to understand it!" he exclaimed.

"Well, it did seem a lot of mystical hogwash when the occult first began to bloom. Remember when you were packing your bag to leave home and I asked if you were going out to Vancouver to consult an old Chinese philosopher? And you said 'You've got it all backwards, Mom. I'm going out to Vancouver *to become* an old Chinese philosopher?' I always thought that was a very snappy come back for a sixteen-year-old kid."

By nightfall, my sense of crisis diminished. Even our silences began to fall naturally. I found myself sorting out subject matter: this will do for now, that can wait for a week; the big questions I'll keep until just before I leave. No confrontations. No precipitous departures. Ben seemed so relaxed, so full of gaiety, I had to keep reminding myself that I was a visiting plenipotentiary to his domain, that I had to conduct myself with due regard for diplomatic protocol, that I was not to mistake the feast of welcome for the real negotiation.

I had come to put my imprimatur upon his adulthood. I had not even begun to consider the trip until I was certain, or as certain as I was capable of being, that I was not going merely to persuade him to give it up and come home. It had taken years of inner debate to overcome the hurt and anguish of his rejection, to outgrow the possessiveness of parenthood. I had come, finally, to listen and to learn, to discover, if I could, what kept him stranded on his island when the whole world lay open to him, if only he would recognize it.

As we moved about the little space, stirring the cooking, handing things back and forth to one another, I was just another mother in the kitchen and Ben was just another young man helping out. Except that it was me helping him, instead of the other way around. When we bumped into one another and said "oops!" I couldn't believe that we were at the end of the world, that it was possible that I had come only to say a last good-bye.

We dined splendidly on venison, sliced and fried and smothered with onions, and steamed cabbage seasoned with sea salt. Fresh pineapple for dessert and white wine with the meal. Ben lit both of his Aladdin oil lamps, to celebrate. I sat in the big armchair, Ben on a three-legged stool he'd finished while we'd spent the afternoon in talk. Through the adjustable hole near the bottom of the Airtight, the embers of a wood fire threw dancing light on the earthen floor. At the far end of the lake a loon laughed raucously.

I lapsed into silence, thinking of my mother's frown when she had handed me a letter she'd received from Ben shortly after he'd moved to Tibbett Lake.

"Dear Grandma," he'd written in his angular, childish hand. "I'm sitting in front of a fire on the shore of my lake.

The moon is shining and it is very quiet, but the music in my head is something my mother used to play. If you hadn't made her practice when she was a little girl, I wouldn't have that music to listen to in my head right now. So I'm writing you to say thank you for making her practice."

"Is that the way to write to a grandmother?" she'd demanded of me. "What does he *mean*, thanking me for making you practice when you were a little girl?" She'd shrugged scornfully when I asked if I could keep the letter. "But don't you remember, Mother, how he used to steal into the living room while I was playing and hide under the piano? How I used to pretend I didn't know he was there?"

"Are you bored, Mom?" Ben asked me now.

"Bored?"

"Well, it isn't exactly what you're used to."

"But that's exactly why I've come, Ben. I've been working terribly hard on my job. I needed a vacation badly."

"Well, you've no idea how I appreciate it. It's good, having company again. I mean, your going to all this . . ."

"Stop!" my mind shouted. "Don't break me up! Don't dissolve me! I'm holding myself together with spit. Don't be grateful. I've come for my own sake more than for yours."

But I said "Never mind, you don't have to worry that I'll outstay my welcome. I'm only hanging around as long as the onions last."

It was time for bed. Of course Ben would walk me up to the Kiosk, or I'd never go. I poured a bit of water into a cup and brushed my teeth for a full fifteen minutes, imitating Ben's waste disposal system with a smart flick of the wrist that earned his praise. He took one of the oil lamps and gave me a battery-powered torch. The lamp shed a soft aura about his figure as he moved through the trees; but the beam from my lamp was straight and far-reaching, and I searched the forest for a pair of yellow eyes to be caught in its spotlight, thought of the tenderness with which the Eskimos bade good-bye to their old people before putting them out to die on an ice floe.

At the Kiosk, Ben lifted his lamp high overhead, scanning the trees, the ground, the plastic tent, both inside and out.

"See?" he said. "There's nothing here!"

"That's just the point!"

"Sleep well," he said, and turned to go. I could not believe he was really going to leave me by myself, but I bit my tongue and watched through the wall as his tall figure receded into the night, merging with the trees. Only when the light inside the little house intensified and I knew he was back inside did I set my torch on the overturned oil-drum. The beam shone straight up, leaving the rest of the Kiosk in darkness.

I took the heirloom watch off first. As the silver chain lisped against the rusty top of the oil drum, I thought I had no need of a badge of identity here. Ben knew perfectly well who I was. Next I removed my boots because the legs of my jeans were too narrow to fit over them. But the mossy floor was likely to be damp and Ben had said I was not to get my feet wet. So I stood on top of the boots while I removed the jacket and the sweaters, hurrying so that I would not get a chill.

My old flannel nightgown felt like a long-lost friend.

I did not have to pee until morning. How could I possibly wait until morning? Would it not be a good idea to establish my territorial imperative with the wolves back up on the mountain? Surely by now they knew I was here. Would urine, being organic, be as serious a pollutant as detergent? Might there be a little hole in the forest floor in which one could discreetly hide a dab of toilet paper?

I reached behind me and flicked off the torch, then zipped the sleeping bag up around my shoulders. Beyond the softly flubbing walls of the Kiosk, it was enormously dark. A star blinked through the shifting treetops. I pictured the terrain beyond, that pillared space, that openness, shutting nothing in—or out. A strong wind looped up from the lake, and my kidneys were bursting.

Carrying the torch like a loaded pistol, I trudged, with bare feet stuck into unlaced boots, what I hoped was a decent distance from the Kiosk. Crouching in the shadow of a giant hemlock, I apologized to it for my acid content.

Now the light in the little house below was extinguished. Around me the stillness was alive. I felt my weight upon the bed, felt my breath drawing in and out through the nostril-sized opening in the sleeping bag, heard the cacophony of my own heartbeat, unable to decide whether the chomping outside the Kiosk was the lake lapping at the shore or the anticipatory salivating of a wolf.

But there was nothing to be done.

If there was a wolf standing outside my door, he would just have to eat a whole lot of nylon before he got to me.

4

I awakened to the clean, vigorous sound of wood being chopped. Raindrops glistened on the roof of the Kiosk. In the high foliage, rainbow-hued sparklers magnified the morning sun. It was nearly ten by the face of my watch, but the floor of the forest was still dark as an open secret. There was no need to hurry. No traffic to dodge, no classes to meet, no papers to grade, no meals to prepare. Congratulating myself on my comfort, my safety, my advantages, I wriggled like an earthworm inside the sleeping bag. In days of yore, only people like Theodore Roosevelt could take such vacations as this . . . no matter that he was president of the United States and Ben was only a squatter. "It just goes to show the democratization of privilege," I said to myself, stretching luxuriously.

Yes, it was marvelous. Who would have thought that a dreamer like Ben could have contrived a solution for his life that reflected so accurately his temperament, his imagination? He'd always defined himself in terms of land, of trees. When he was a buck-toothed Boy Scout, and when Gilly was a Girl Scout in the same town, he'd asked us if, instead of a fountain pen for his thirteenth birthday, we might consider giving him a little piece of land all his own, where he could save all the trees.

Now he had it, in a manner of speaking. He'd found a way of living in the most beautiful setting in North America, free of charge.

It was altogether in keeping with the romantic faith in Nature as Healer, Nature as Teacher, Nature as Shaper of Men. A nineteenth-century notion, to be sure, implying that humans were the highest manifestation of divine will, that birth into the real world was a fall from grace which nature, properly embraced, could redeem. Ben had merely set the clock back a hundred years, scratched two world wars and the atom bomb out of his consciousness. Yes, Lord Baden-Powell would have been thrilled if he had lived to see it, and so would Rudyard Kipling. We, too, had believed in the salutory effects of nature. Like most of the city-born, we always kept a bird book on the shelf above the kitchen sink, took the reforestation of our front lawn with dead earnestness, had even gone a-hunting for a piece of wild land to buy for Ben, in the Adirondacks. Within commuting distance of suburbia.

Unfortunately, history had interrupted our suburban idyll. We never bought that piece of land for Ben. The war in Vietnam was just beginning when he was fourteen. There were no doves to denounce it then, no parades of half a million down in Washington. There was only fear and a despairing silence. To guilt-tormented Americans with draft-age sons, Canada looked like heaven. When Ben's father was offered a good job in Montreal, we persuaded one another that we were not copping-out, packed suburbia in, and, instead of a piece of wild land, we gave Ben a whole new country.

It was hard to be an American in Canada, then. Hard for us, uncomfortable for the younger children, but nearly impossible for fourteen-year-old Ben. Nonconformists were anathema in Canadian schools. His classmates called him a "baby-bomber" and burned an American flag in the school yard. But when he wore antiwar buttons to school, they mobbed him for being a Communist.

He hated school and made very few friends. Four months before he was supposed to graduate and wouldn't, couldn't, he announced that he was leaving for Vancouver. Winter didn't last so long in Vancouver, he said.

Now I could see how logical it was, an extrapolation of the same suburban impulse to flee complexity and conflict, to start all over again in the innocent bosom of nature. And now, for the millionth time, my mind spiraled down to the final scene of Ben's derailment. Like the tip of a tongue worrying an aching tooth, I searched it over once again.

"If you don't hurry up, Ben, you're going to miss the train for running away from home!" I'd said in a well-modulated voice as he stuffed the last pair of socks into his backpack. No Mrs. Portnoy, I. Not one of your possessive, domineering, middle-class mothers. Not a person to use my anxiety as a weapon of emotional oppression. I believed in self-determination, even for mixed-up sixteen-year-olds.

His father drove him down to the railroad terminal, supervised the purchase of a one-way ticket to Vancouver out of the little cache of birthday checks we called "Ben's college fund." He explained to Ben carefully how to avail himself of the resources of the Traveler's Aid Society, the public library, the police department, the emergency rooms of hospitals, and the long distance telephone, and helped Ben load his canvas bag onto the train.

Wiping the tears from my cheeks with his thumbs, Hal said to me, "He'll be home in a couple of months. He's got to get it out of his system. Boys are like that."

Could Ben have thought that because we were cool we didn't care?

Every time we were sure he was about to give it up and come back home, he moved farther north, deeper into the wilderness. We sent him plane fare. At first he came home for two or three weeks at a time, usually months after we expected him. He was amiable but distant, and when we'd ask him "What are you going to *do?*" he'd reply, "Just what I am doing." "But what are you going to *be?*" "Just what I already am."

As the years went by, the visits grew less frequent and the letters grew shorter and less coherent. He began to convert our checks into brown rice and soy beans. Cosmic energy was what he wrote to us about, and spirals of consciousness, the kind of things that would have driven Lord Baden-Powell out of his Victorian mind.

A civil libertarian friend of ours suggested, "If he were my son, I'd go up there and bring him home in handcuffs."

Others wondered why we did not dispatch a psychiatrist to go and talk him out of it. Apart from the possibility that a really thoughtful psychiatrist might join him instead of treat him, who was to say that someone who'd spent twenty-five years passing examinations in order to qualify for intimate human discourse was better adapted to the insanity of contemporary life than Ben?

Of those who believed that we were lying, covering up while Ben sweated out amnesty as a draft resister, I do not speak. If the draft had ever reached his number he would probably have become a conscientious objector. But he was never called.

So why had he not come back home when the war was over? The rest of the family had left Canada long before. He could have come back at any time.

Which brought me right back to where I started. If I had not found a key to the puzzle in six years, I was not going to find it lying in bed on a morning in May.

Moreover it was day, and I was, as yet, uneaten.

Inside the house, oatmeal bubbled on the propane stove and the coffee pot on the Airtight was hot and fragrant. Ben was a little way off, chopping wood, and I looked about for some way to make myself useful. I could fill the water bucket.

There was an echo of old violence in the cataclysm of rock and timber above the pool. The water under the log bridge was a swirl of bubbles and whirlpools, full of life and speech. But underneath my feet the current ran deep and still and scarcely stirred the overhanging ferns. A dragonfly with iridescent wings poked at the space and darted away. I hesitated, unwilling to invade the mystery of the place with my bucket, and was truly astounded when the substance I drew out of that wild and secret place turned out to be ordinary water.

Ben followed me into the house, his arms laden with firewood. His cheeks were ruddy and his eyes still puffy with morning.

"Sleep well?" he asked, and kissed me glancingly on

the cheek.

"Wonderfully. And you?"

"Took a couple of hours but I did fall asleep, finally. I'm not used to going to bed so early."

I wondered how he had the courage to get out of bed at all when there was no one needing him. How did he shoulder the daily burden of organizing his time? How did he plan for high points and low points, structure the rhythm of his existence?

"What do you do that keeps you up so late at night?"

"Read," he replied. "Work. Think about the family." And spooned the oatmeal into bowls.

After breakfast, there was no longer any way of circumventing the facility. It began to rain again and the wind was swooping up from the lake. While Ben was occupied under the plastic tent, I slipped out the back door, crossed the brook, and climbed the rough slope, stepping cautiously over tangled vines and boulders covered with pale green lichen. The contours of the little house below were scarcely visible through the trees. As I climbed the rootsteps of the monolithic stump, my foot slipped and the bark I grasped disintegrated in my fingers. My longjohns were designed with a trap door, and I had to remove one pant leg to haul my jeans around in front of me. I hopped around like a circus elephant, trying to keep my right sock dry and clear of the platform, and nearly fell through the opening. But I learned what the dumbest animal understands at birth: nature has arranged the body in such a way as to make such heroic measures wholly irrelevant. It was no small revelation; in its light, civilization appeared more of a disabler than I'd ever suspected. Things have come to a pretty pass when a person doesn't even know the exact location of their own asshole.

It rained all morning, a heavy, steady downpour. Heavy mist lay over the lake. The whole scene contracted, shrank to the size of the fire in the Airtight and the sound of the wood planer as Ben worked at the outdoor bench.

"I've got an idea," I said. "I'd like to make you a little handle out of wood, to lift the lid off the Airtight. You burn your fingers every time you put wood in the stove."

Ben gave me a fine length of cedar and his best penknife, and set me to whittling beside the stove. "That's the greatest knife," he said. "Dad gave it to me. I nearly lost it last fall. I was out on Tibbett Lake, fishing, and I dropped it into about thirty feet of water. I just couldn't afford to lose it, so I went back the next day with a magnet at the end of my fishing line and pulled it right up. Nothing ever gets lost around here."

It was very pleasant just to sit beside the stove and carve. I shaped the new tool cunningly, with a twist at the tip for prying up the stove lid and a stout handle with a groove for the thumb. The small, red knife in my hand was sharp, a splendid tool. And as the lid-handle began to take shape, it seemed to me that there was great virtue in Hal's way—to give our children the very best tools he could find and allow them to cut their own way through the snares and tangles of life. I wished that I could leave it at that. But it wasn't in me to be so objective. It was more than six years since Ben had left home and I still missed him. We all missed him. Ben was the elusive exception in our lives, the one who added a different dimension. Around the table at every birthday and every holiday, it was always said "Well, everybody's here. Except for Ben." Did he know that? Oh, Ben, do you know that?

By early afternoon the rain stopped, and Ben said,

"Come on, let's go for a walk in the woods. I want to show you where you're at. We'll take a look at Nootka Creek."

I was glad, by then, to get out, to shift the scenery in my mind. Besides, the moment the sun came out, the interior of the house became stuffy as a steam bath.

It was strenuous exercise, scrambling over hurdles, jumping from rock to rock, following Ben along an invisible path. But I wouldn't let him help me, wouldn't concede that much dependence upon him. "I can do it myself," I said, just the way he used to say those words to me when he was a little boy. "Don't, Mom. I can do it by myself."

Where the forest deepened we came upon a rock ledge. Under its shadowed flank a thin stream of water splashed on a platform of flat granite. "I'm going to build a sauna here," Ben said. "Won't it be great?"

Sitting in a sauna seemed a gloomy sort of pastime if there was no one around to complain to about the heat. "Wouldn't it be dangerous to build a fire in here, to heat the rocks?"

"Oh, come on, Mom. Think I don't know how to handle fire?"

He showed me what fire had already done to his forest, how many great trees were charred around the base, how much broken charcoal lay upon the ground. The old loggers used to set the torch to a place when they cleared out, so as not to leave anything over for the competition. I saw the remains of an old trestle, a huge, rotting structure overgrown with vines and ferns, awesome in its collapse. Young boys used to run alongside the logs and throw foul-smelling grease on the skids to ease the timber down the mountain to the lake. They used donkey engines for power and the sparks, too, ignited fires.

For every mammoth stump clutching the hillside, a dozen younger trees had grown back, none of them comparable in proportion to the virgin growth. Ben showed me the notches in the stumps, well over my head, some notched in a dozen places, where springboards were inserted like spokes from the hub of a wheel, and loggers stood, sawing in pairs, with ten-foot blades.

We moved deeper in, crawling under snags as thick as a man was tall. Ferns sprouted from bodies of trees half a millenium into disintegration, long green tongues of moss hanging from their flanks like drapery. Wispy green beards of moss hung from the lower branches of standing trees, like reflections of the thin ferns sprouting from the forest floor. Ben showed me the difference between cedar and balsam, spruce and Douglas fir. Reaching for light, these trees had grown halfway to heaven, so thick around that three men with outstretched arms could not have embraced them.

Except for a brilliant patch emblazoning a lofty trunk with a shield of lion-colored sunlight, the forest was shrouded and dim. The earth was strange, as well; a thin membrane of soil, like web-footing covering the bones and tendons of protruding roots. As if time were measured here in eons, and the trees were in the process of evolving into giant amphibians. Merely to look required courage. I thought of Ben entering this forest alone for the first time, ears cocked, breath short, heart pounding, summoning up a magic of his own to match the power of the woods.

He led the way into a dense growth and paused before a fallen cedar as thick at the base as he was tall. Fingering the bark as if it were the fabric of the tree's skirt, he said, "Look how straight it is," and asked me to sight it along its

length. It seemed too great a familiarity, almost an imperti-
nence, to subject so noble a form to human appraisal. The
tree did not have to be straight to earn my respect. So I
moved toward the middle where the top was only as high
as my waist and, clinging to the vines that pinned it to the
earth, I hoisted myself up. There were chisel marks for
thirty or forty feet along the spine. My own voice startled
me in that penetrating stillness. "Yes, Ben, it's straight as
a die."

"You see? It hardly had any lower branches." He
spoke softly, as if not to rouse the slumbering spirits surrounding us. "Very unusual for a tree to grow to this size
in such a thick forest. All its energy went into vertical
growth. When the Indians discovered a tree like this, they'd
have a big celebration. If it was standing, they'd cut away
all the trees in the line of fall and cushion the ground with
cedar bark. Then they'd sing to it and pray for a soft, easy
fall so it wouldn't crack, going down. " 'Come on, tree,'
they'd sing, 'you really do want to become a dug-out
canoe.' " He chuckled with delight in the story. "They'd
sing the same thing to whales before they harpooned them.
'Come on, whale dear, you know you want us to get you!' "

"Are there whales in Dyer Strait?"

"Sure. They come down every spring."

"How'd you find out all that stuff about the Indians?
Are there any Indians living here now?"

"No. I read it in a book over at the Civic Center, on
Capaswap. We've got a great public library there. But an
old Indian down on a reservation near Victoria showed me
how to burn out a tree core for a dugout. You drive dyed
plugs in from the outside, to get the thickness even. When
you hit the color, you know you've cut deep enough. The

guys who built the canoes were holy men among the Nootka. Had to keep their hair tied up all the time they were carving, because if a single hair fell on the ground a crack would appear in the wood. They couldn't look at women, even think about women, when they were working. If they were impure, even in their thoughts, rotten spots would turn up in the wood."

"Hmmm."

Ben climbed up and we sat on the tree's back, side by side, resting.

"Did you make those chisel marks?"

"Uh-huh," he said. "I wrote you about this tree once."

My heart sank.

Long ago, Ben had written me a joyful, enthusiastic letter describing his discovery of this very tree. "Imagine!" he wrote, "Sixty feet of perfectly clear cedar! I'm going to carve a dugout and sail it up the coast to Alaska."

He'd really intended to do it. The chisel marks were testimony. Without the chanting, without the rituals, without the traditions, without a community to give the action substance or meaning. Simply by a determined act of his imagination.

"Even if you could have carved a canoe by yourself, how could you have gotten it down to water?"

"Good, Mom. Very good. Now you're beginning to think like a logger," he said. "That was the whole trouble. The Indians used to roll the carved part out of the forest on a raft of logs. It wasn't ever allowed to touch the earth. They didn't put in the bows until just before the launching. That was where the Yankee Clippers got the design. From the Nootka. Anyhow, I brought Dale over to see it. We tried for a couple of days to figure out some way to take it out, but we couldn't. It would take at least ten guys." He regarded the log with sorrow, then pointed to a cut deep into the thickness of the trunk. "Since then, I've been cutting off small pieces as I need them," he said. "It's wonderful wood."

He spoke as if it were a desecration forced upon him by cold logic, and it would have taken a harder heart than mine not to grieve with him.

Now we moved crosswise to the mountain's slope and began to descend again. Ben stopped to show me an enormous log which had fallen across the bed of a little brook. A few rusted tin cans lay about. He pointed to a stretched triangle of canvas beneath the log.

"Fellow named Harry Fox lived here last fall," he said. "Used the place as a hideout for some crazy, get-rich-quick scheme. He hated it here. I used to hear him in the middle of the night—he'd scream at the wolves, shoot off his gun, curse like a maniac. Look! It fell right smack in the middle of his ridgepole. Crushed his cast-iron stove like a tin cup. A tree like that could have been waiting for two hundred years for the right moment to topple over!"

I was afraid to ask him what had happened to Harry, afraid he was still with us, pinned under the tree.

"If he'd stayed here one more hour, one more hour, imagine! The tree would have got him. Squashed him like a bug."

"What made him leave? Vibrations?"

"No, there was a big hailstorm that morning. He had a garden down near the delta and the storm wiped the whole thing out. I guess it was the last straw. He cleared out in such a hurry, he left a lot of stuff behind. I found a package of letters. The last one was one he'd written him-

self, to his father, detailing a scheme for beating the odds
at Las Vegas. He never mailed it. I thought I ought to mail
it for him but, well, I don't get down to Campbell River
that often myself, and after a while it seemed foolish. He
left a good string hammock behind. I made a rack for drying deer jerky out of it."

We reached Nootka Creek, a six-foot-wide stream with
a shifting sand bar, which Ben bent to study at length.
"Not too bad yet," he observed. About thirty feet from its
banks, there were bright red ribbons tied around the
trunks of the trees. "They're required to leave a margin
thirty feet wide on either side of a stream, by law," he said,
"to protect the fish. But one good westerly and the whole
screen will fall down and choke the creek. Unless the whole
forest stands, acts as a buffer, the stream's finished. We sent
a letter to the Forestry Service about a month ago, protesting. They've started building the road across it, farther up,
so maybe the letter did some good. But the water's already
starting to cloud up. . . ."

"Who's we?"

"Me and Dale Finn. He's good at dealing with bureaucrats."

"And who's 'they'?"

"The Company. The logging company. They've got a
lease to all the lumber on Proctor's Island. And about five
other islands around here. They were the ones got the
Forestry Service to burn down the place I was in before
this."

"They want to cut this whole place down? And what's
going to happen to you when they do?"

"That's what the meeting's about, partly. The one I
want you to stay for. We're supposed to spend a whole day

with this old guy, Swen Mohring. He's been with the Company twenty-five years. Used to be a camp supervisor. Not a bad guy. He's really got the interests of the woods at heart."

I turned away, lest Ben detect my disbelieving smile.

A grassy meadow opened up at the edge of the woods. It was flooded, now, with the mellow sunlight of late afternoon. Willow trees grazed the meandering delta of Nootka Creek; gay little pink and yellow flowers dotted the grass. Fiddlehead ferns grew in abundance in this unexpected province of innocence and delight, and Ben picked enough to fill his old woolen tuque. "Fiddleheads are great with venison," he said. "All this food, just five minutes from home."

Then he stooped and picked up a tuft of grizzled fur.

"Wolf got a deer here," he said.

". . . how many months ago, would you say?"

"Months? I'd say it was within the last three days. You're standing on the hip bone."

Not any more, I wasn't.

"See? Fresh wolf spoor. They always take a shit to celebrate a kill."

I felt myself falter, felt my strength ebb. Ben had already crossed the creek, carelessly, in a single leap. "Ben?" I said to his back. "May I have your hand?"

"Sorry, Mom," he said, doubling back across the water. "I didn't think you wanted . . . I mean, you're so . . . independent now."

5

The trip caught up with me the next day. I awoke tired and depressed and wished I were back home in my own bed, wondered how the rest of my family was faring in my absence. "Don't stay away too long, Mom," my young daughter had whispered in my ear. "Dad hardly ever smiles when you're not home."

She hadn't said it to be cruel, she said it because she felt abandoned. All four of my children must have felt abandoned as they smiled and waved me good-bye. They waited for my vacations nearly as much as they did for their own, counted on our intimate conversations, coming into my book-lined study one after another to unburden their hearts and to fortify mine. "What's Ben ever done for this family, that she'd go off and leave all of us just to see him?" they must have asked themselves.

Children have their own way of measuring love. I'd

never been able to share with them the depth of my doubts about Ben. I had no words with which to describe to them the thread that bound me to this son. I scarcely had words to describe it to myself. It would have sounded pious, or mystic, or sentimental to say I believed that his connectedness to life depended, in some obscure way, upon me; that I was his last chance; that unless I affirmed his existence, he might slip out of it, irrevocably. I had waited and waited and waited, hoping he would return of his own accord, and I could wait no longer. It was going on the seventh year.

"You don't look so good this morning," Ben said when we met in the house. "Didn't you sleep? Were you cold?"

"I'm all right, Ben. I'm just not used to walking so much."

"You used to walk a lot. We always went for walks. Is it on account of your job?"

"Partly. There just doesn't seem to be as much time as there used to be. It's not only me. Nobody walks. Even the Fuller Brush men come in cars. About the only people who walk are the children, going to school and coming home. And Girl Scouts who ring the bell and try to sell you stale chocolate peppermint cookies. You and Gilly never sold cookies when you were in the Scouts. Remember when you went camping on the Appalachian Trail at ten below zero, and I drove up the next day with the station wagon full of groceries?"

"Never forget it!" he said. And smiled wanly when I added, "Things haven't changed that much, have they?"

He fixed as fancy a breakfast as a person could fix without eggs or bacon or orange juice or toast. I hadn't thought to bring along bread and Ben was out of flour. He apologized for this, said that in a few days we would go and visit Gilly. He would swap a chunk of venison for flour and a little more coffee, and maybe a jar of cooking oil since his supply was running low. "A person is always welcome when they bring meat," he said.

"Is it far, to Gilly's?"

"About two hours, in good weather. We'll wait until you get your energy back. There's no hurry."

"Is she happy with this guy?"

"I don't know, Mom. I can't get involved. When I see people in pain I say to them, here's a band-aid. Take care of yourself. Don't ask me for anything. I can't help you. Christ! Everybody's in pain. You can't do anything about it!"

I was not in a position to contradict him about Gilly, for I had offered her a large band-aid once myself, and had suffered a debacle! She wasn't a run-of-the-mill person, not even when she was twelve, when she and Ben hid together on the low branch of a big pine tree in our back yard, sharing a smoke. She was short and fair-skinned, with curly, red hair. She wore thick eyeglasses and a plaid, wool jumper, the school uniform of an institution in town which Ben always called "the Convent of the Scared Heart." She was a boarder, an only child whose mother was a dancer on her fourth marriage.

She was very wary of me then. Whenever I came into a room she would turn into a deaf-mute. "What were you talking about?" I once asked Ben, irritated by her mistrust. "Tolkien. Gilly's really into Tolkien. We were talking about Middle Earth. You really ought to read Tolkien, Mom." Perhaps I should have. Perhaps if I had, I'd have understood more than I did now what went on inside Ben's head.

Fixing breakfast, Ben bustled around the little house, trying to cheer me up. He twisted a pair of pipe cleaners into the shape of eyeglasses, placed them over his nose, and scrutinized a tiny calendar tacked to a beam—one of those insurance man's calendars that squeeze 365 days onto a space two-and-a-half inches long and an inch-and-a-quarter high. Turning back toward the workbench and peering over the top of the frames, the way I did, he plucked a stubby pencil from a tin can and drew three little crosses on the calendar. It pleased him when I giggled.

"You've been here three days and I forgot to mark my calendar. I usually mark the calendar the first thing every morning."

"In expectation of what?" I wondered, but did not ask.

"Time sure flies, when you've got company," he added.

After breakfast and the facility, I told Ben that I would go down to the little beach and sit by the water for awhile. I did not want him to knock himself out trying to entertain me. Besides, it was a beautiful morning and the sun was shining brightly. "You do whatever you have to, Ben. I don't want to interfere with your work."

The beach was about twenty feet long, sandy and pebbled, bounded on the left by the fallen log, two-thirds of which lay in shallow water. There was room on the dry part for five lengths of me, placed end to end. The kayak, a single-seater, slept on the sand with its eyes open. Just beyond it stood a huge old stump, charred at the top, with berry bushes and long grass fringing its crown. A fresh breeze danced over the lake, making trails of chiffon on the sparkling surface. The dark hills embracing it lay, fold upon fold, massive and fixed. Beyond them rose the white peaks of Vancouver Island's mountain range, the highest of them encircled at the base by a ring of clouds.

I climbed up on the log and regarded Ben's scenery, pretty as a travel poster and just as vacant. Somewhere in those hills lived a girl who loved Ben enough to follow him to the end of nowhere. It was a great opening shot, this panorama, except that the actors were mute and scattered, and the director had lost the script.

When the sharply sloping log beneath my butt grew cold and damp, I lay down as if it were a slant board and I was giving my circulation a change of direction. I clasped my hands over my stomach, braced myself against the curving surface with my elbows, nailing myself to the mast. But as soon as I relaxed, I rolled off.

Better, I thought, to sit near the stump. There was a small canvas seat pad in the kayak, and I made a roost for myself between two of the stump's protruding knees. A yard beyond the yellow toes of my boots, a colony of tadpoles rocked in a bubbly frill of foam, forming a brown ribbon at the water's edge. Between two other knees of the stump a spider was hard at work completing a windproof web. Even in its last extremity, the stump nurtured the fragile life of other species of flora and fauna. While cardboard calendars floated in my brain, I leaned against its great gray chest and felt as if I were resting in the lap of my own grandfather.

My silence, my inertia must have bothered Ben. He was not accustomed to seeing me idle. "You're the most organized person I ever knew," he used to say to me, half in reproach, when I'd line up a sequence of jobs for myself. Long before he left home I'd stopped lining up a sequence of jobs for him. I only served as a reverse model for him in this regard.

So it did not surprise me when he came down to the

beach to see what I was doing. He brought along the leg of a third chair and squatted on the sand, Indian fashion, while he whittled a square shape out of a round one.

"Explain to me about this meeting you want me to go to, Ben," I said. "Tell me about your work."

He had never been good at organizing data. His way of seeing things always rested on some zany insight into personality, which set him off into wildly extrapolated fantasy, jokes. But he tried to be serious, to answer my questions one after the other, starting with who actually owned all this scenery.

Most of the islands in Dyer Strait, and a very large part of the rest of British Columbia, were known as crown lands, he said, a leftover term from the days when Canada was still a dominion of the British Empire and anything that was not in private hands belonged, in theory, to the monarch, Queen Elizabeth. Now that Canada was an independent country, these lands belonged to the public and were administered by the provincial government through various agencies such as the Fish and Wildlife Service, the Forestry Service and so on. "So . . . I'm part of the public, aren't I?" he said.

"But is it the government that's cutting all the timber?"

"No, the government leased it to the Company, and they do all the cutting."

"The same outfit that has those lovely commercials on TV, with all the biologists, and forest murmurings in the background?"

"Yeah. Bastards. Fools. All except for Swen. He's a nice guy. The thing is that the bureaucrats down in Vancouver don't know anything about what goes on up here.

They sit in their dumb offices and write memorandums to each other. Fish and Wildlife doesn't talk to Forestry, Forestry doesn't talk to Immigration, Immigration doesn't talk to Manpower, and the whole place goes haywire."

I knew that Ben earned a little money from time to time by splitting "shakes." "Shakes" was the local word for cedar shingles, slices of straight-grained, weatherproof wood used for siding or roofing materials; they increased the price of any suburban ranch house to which they were fastened by several thousand dollars. But I did not know where the shake-splitting was done, or when, or how they were sold, or whether Ben actually had any legal claim to the product.

"We've got a minor timber lease. That means that we can't cut a tree down, but we can make shakes out of any cedar that's already on the ground. There's millions of windfalls. They're choking up the woods."

"What you need here is another CCC."

"What's the CCC?"

"During the depression the government rounded up thousands of unemployed young men and sent them out to clean up the forests. The Civilian Conservation Corps. When Roosevelt was president."

"Oh," he said, and I could see from his face that he thought I was talking about right after the Civil War.

"I hope I'm not keeping you from working, by being here?"

"Oh, no! We work whenever we feel like it. In fact, there's about a two-year accumulation of shakes around Capaswap Lake, waiting to be shipped out."

"You're going to negotiate with this man, Swen? About the price?"

"Jesus, no, Mom! We've got a lot more important things to talk to him about. Why do you always think about money?"

Time to take another tack.

"Is Gilly part of the group? Does she split shakes too?"

"Yeah, she's a member, but she doesn't do much. All you have to do to belong to Coastal Environment Cooperative is guarantee to spend at least one month a year on Proctor's Island and chip in twenty-five dollars. Dale's the president. The lease is in his name. I'm the treasurer."

"The treasurer?"

He grinned. "Don't worry. There isn't any money in the treasury."

It was better than I thought. He did belong to something. There was a framework, an economy of sorts, even if it was only a cottage industry. Not that there had not been other organizations in the background of Ben's life in western Canada. When he lived at Casin Point, on another island in Dyer Strait, but further south, in the old generator shack (I now knew), we addressed his mail in care of Cosmic Logging. Maybe the changes in name reflected the ascendency of ecological concern over the occult. If so, it was a step in the right direction.

"What was the Institute of Containerology, Ben?" That was the place to which we sent mail when he lived in Vancouver, in the old garage. It sounded to me like an illegitimate offspring of Buckminster Fuller. "I never understood about that."

"Most of the people in it were on public welfare. The city made goofy jobs. They had a housing project on the books called False Creek, and they used to send some of us down there to rake water."

I stared out over the lake for a long time, working up courage to ask him "Were you ever on relief, Ben?"

"No," he said, "Not that I have anything against it. I'm not above taking relief. One time I got as far as the social worker's desk, but I couldn't sign the application. I don't know why. So I sold her a drawing instead, for twenty bucks, and I came back up here."

"I'm glad, Ben."

"I know," he said. And got up to fetch a steel file for rounding off his chair leg.

I still didn't understand what the meeting with Swen was supposed to be about; Ben didn't seem to have a clear idea about it either. Maybe he just thought of it as a chance to have a nice, long heart-to-heart talk with a father figure. It didn't matter enough, to me, to pursue it further. I had no inclination to get down to basics with Ben; not yet, for, before we were five sentences into any subject, we arrived at a parting of the ways. Moreover, in the back of my mind, I'd always had a secret hope that something big and impersonal, like the inexorable logic of economics, would force Ben out of his retreat. If that did it, it would take the onus off me.

I was relieved when he asked me to look at a sweater I'd made for him several years before. He'd stored it for the summer in an airtight tin, but a mouse had eaten a hole, twice its own size, clear through the chest to the back. Ben was lavish in praise of my craftsmanship, asserted that the sweater was not only warm but waterproof, that it had cured him of a bad cold last year, that in addition to its magical and medicinal qualities it was also nutritious. "The mouse died of suffocation," he claimed stoutly, "and not of indigestion."

I was happy to play mother instead of critic and interrogator, and took the matter under study. The holes were far too large to be darned. What they required, I decided, was the knitting of two large squares and the careful insertion of them into the fabric. "Got any yarn?"

"No, but Gilly has. She's got tons of wool, but she never makes anything out of it. She'll be glad to give you some."

"How about you let me unravel your raggedy tuque? The color is about right."

"Never!" he cried, seizing his head with both hands. "This is my best hat!"

"Jesse just sent you a beautiful, new red one!"

"Makes no difference. You can't have my hat."

He'd taken the sweater out of the suitcase under the workbench, and saw me eyeing his notebook covetously. "Will you let me read it before I leave?"

"If you insist," he replied, shutting the case and poking it back into the space below the bench.

A hearty lunch revived me. Ben brewed up a large pot of Labrador tea, the leaf of a berry brush that grew on the island. It had a smoky taste, a little like Earl Grey's, and Ben said it was very good for the circulation. We consumed a couple of oranges and finished the cottage cheese, richly invested with raisins.

While Ben chipped and planed another chair leg at his workbench, I returned to my roost at the beach with his sewing kit, trimming the loose threads of the sweater and binding them, one at a time, to the fabric. A plane droned by, high overhead, and far off in the direction of Nootka Creek I heard a dull thud, like a muffled explosion. Later, Ben told me it was the Company, dynamiting another stretch of the new road. Apart from this it was incredibly quiet. Not even a fly buzzed by. From time to time a couple of gulls screamed, and a raven flew over, croaking. I watched an eagle flapping slowly and deliberately toward a roost on the mountain behind me, but it passed beyond my sight before I got a really good look. Halfway through the sweater, a great lassitude overcame me and I stretched out on the sand and tried to nap in the sunshine. But it was too cold and too damp, so I went back to the Kiosk, hoping to sleep it off.

It wasn't very comfortable in the Kiosk either. I felt uneasy, unresolved, far away from Ben. Our conversations raised more questions than they answered. We were like two boxers in a ring, sparring with one another, taking pokes at the territory between us, and withdrawing as soon as we were in danger of making contact.

Ben was on the third leg of the new chair when I gave up the Kiosk and returned to the clearing, to sit on his workbench and watch him. He was very handy with tools. When he was little, he used to make all sorts of fantastic structures that he called "concraptions." Elaborate arrangements of string, yarn, rubber bands, tape, rope, wire. He'd tie the most unlikely things together: chair legs to door knobs, door knobs to window shades, window shades to lamp cords; devices for remote control so that he could regulate his environment without having to participate in it visibly. Running through the house with my arms full of babies, I always had to be on guard lest I fall over one of his concraptions.

When he grew older, the constructions matured, too. He made a beautiful model of one of Leonardo Da Vinci's bridges. Ricky was crazy about that bridge and still kept it on his window sill.

Ben's most memorable concraption was the giraffe he

made for Halloween. He figured out a way of rigging strings along a twelve-foot length of wood so he could open and close the giraffe's mouth from the base of its neck. His father and I stayed up most of the night helping him finish the costume. I sewed a head for it and stuffed it with foam rubber. It had heavy woolen eyelashes and a lolling tongue of red felt. My husband helped Ben with the basic carpentry. I made a great point of the necessity of working the mouth with one hand, so Ben would be able to carry his UNICEF can along. "You can ask for dollar bills, pick them up with the giraffe's mouth," I said. He did collect a lot of money for the starving children of the world, and he won first prize at school for the costume. It was the only time he'd ever come in first in anything.

"Remember Giraffe?" I asked him now. He looked up, startled.

"Is he still under the cellar stairs?" He did a fine imitation of a giraffe when I said yes, of course. "Hot dog!" he exclaimed. "Good old Giraffe! I really missed Giraffe when we moved to Montreal."

"We should have taken him along, but there was so much other stuff to put on the van. Yes, he's a bit dusty, but he's still leaning up in the corner."

It could have been that memories of a happy childhood would have opened the floodgates, that one thing would have led to another, that the day would have ended with Ben's packing his bags and coming back home with me. But things like that only happen in old-fashioned novels. This was real life. The great trees around us were real trees, the water lapping against the shore was real water, deep and turbid, and the distance between Ben and me would have given Leonardo Da Vinci pause.

We made it through the afternoon in limping conversation, a series of false starts and sudden stops. I was not highly amused when, toward evening, a shadow flitted across the dirt floor of the little house and the teapot on the propane stove toppled over, apparently of its own accord. "It's my resident toad, Gussie," Ben said, restoring the teapot to position. "She eats all the mosquito larvae. Doesn't see very well in the dark. I worry she'll scald herself some day."

We had venison again for dinner, this time with potatoes and carrots. Ben sliced the meat and fried it in a skillet in a little oil. "Unless you eat lean meat with oil, you lose weight on it. It's pure protein, burns up all your fat."

It was too early to go to bed and too dark to work on the sweater by lamplight. So when dinner was cleared away, I took out my stove handle and the pen knife and whittled by the Airtight.

"Are you comfortable there, Mom?" Ben asked me. "Are you keeping your feet dry?"

"I'm as comfortable as I'd be in our own living room," I said, having been, at certain times, extremely uncomfortable in my own living room.

"That's a very great compliment," he said. "But I wish I'd put in a wooden floor before you came. Trouble is, a person's energy gets awfully low here in the winter. Got to keep yourself pretty quiet when there's not much food." His face grew soft in the lamplight. He looked confessional, and I grew afraid.

"And you're never too lonely here, Ben?"

"I had a pretty bad time this past winter," he said. "Nobody else stayed. I didn't see anybody else for about three months. Sometimes it got so quiet I wondered if the whole world had come to a stop. Then I'd hear a whiff of a power saw from over the mountains, or a plane would fly past. Those were big events for me. Around the beginning of March it got really bad. The lake started melting and I couldn't walk across any more, and I couldn't use a boat either.

"When the moon was half full, I really felt as if I had to split. The lake was half mushy ice, half clear water. Everything seemed to be waxing. I had to get out of my old space, to get mobile again. So I took a beat-up, old skiff, the one lying down near the creek, and used it like a hammer to break the ice. I got to open water all right. Made up my mind to go north to Chilicote Channel. There's a post office over there, and a little store. I was out of tobacco, low on matches and propane gas. I'd bought things on credit from them before. I had less than a dollar on me, but I knew the people. They came up from the States during the Vietnam War, became Canadian citizens so they could run the post office. You can't hold a government job unless you're a citizen."

If he was in such bad shape, why hadn't he written? Phoned? Why had he not told us? It must have been in March. It was March when I finally made up my mind to come here. Maybe I got his message, four thousand miles away.

"If Chilicote Channel is on the coast of Proctor's Island, shouldn't we send your mail there? Isn't it nearer than Campbell River?"

"It *is* nearer, but it's hard to get to overland. Most of their business comes from coastal steamers. I can usually get there in one day's travel, but I had to stop a few miles this side. There's a small lake to cross. A guy who used to live here had a row boat hidden in the bushes, so I slept in it. Covered up with balsam boughs, and a piece of old blanket he'd left in the boat. I must have looked pretty woolly when I finally got there.

"I *know* the old man saw me coming out of the woods," Ben said bitterly. "He only pretended that he didn't see me. He was talking to a cash customer and he turned the other way. I asked his son for a pack of cigarettes and he says to me, 'I quit smoking. Why can't you?'

"I got so mad I turned around and went back home. Just did without."

I cast about wildly for a way to respond to his story but could find none. All that pain, and nothing resolved.

"A couple of weeks later, Dale ran into the old man down in Campbell River. He asked for me, asked Dale to tell me he was sorry he couldn't have given me credit at the time. He had a package for me. Sea and Air Transport had forwarded it. So I went. He nearly fell over himself, wanted me to stay to dinner, taste his home-baked bread. 'Look who's here!' he yells to his wife, 'the boy who gets books from New York!' It was sad, how badly he wanted to be friends."

"How did he know there were books in the package?"

"It said so on the package. You ought to know. You sent them. He was dying to know what they were, so after a while I opened it up. 'Fine books!' he says, looking over my shoulder. I could see he was tickled to know I came from an intellectual family."

"And so you're good friends again. Well, it's nice to know you weren't the only human being on the island this winter, after all."

"No," he said, his lips drawn in a straight line, "we are

not good friends. I'll never go back there again. He knew that I always paid my debts."

I'd never seen this side of Ben before, this hauteur, this icy unforgiveness. One strike, and the man was *out*. It should have given me a clue, but I was too upset to take it.

"Well, all the same, Ben," I said lamely, "you've done an awful lot in the past two years. It's a wonderful place you've fixed up for yourself."

"Thanks," he said grimly, "but the next place I build is going to be twice as big."

". . . If only it weren't so far away! If only it didn't cost so much to get here. We could . . ."

"Did it cost a lot?" he interrupted me, laying his sharp chisel down on the bench beside him. He knew the price of air fare as well as I. He knew that my coming meant postponing fixing the roof, was wedged into my slim finances before college costs for the younger children ate up the surplus next year; that after this there would be nothing left over to lavish on travel for any of us. And I knew that he was offering me his head to lay the blame upon for a needless expense. But I'd calculated the cost long before I made the trip, calculated everything—the groceries, the taxis, the clothing, the camping gear, the bus fare. He had lived for two years on what it cost me to come here.

"It was as expensive as hell, Ben," I replied, and gave him the grand total, exactly to the penny.

He rose from his high perch, unfolding his long legs stiffly, like a heron. "Well . . ." he said with asperity, "I'll do my best to give you your money's worth, for your vacation." And kicked his way out through the door flap, into the darkness.

I dug furiously at the stove stick, hating him and hating myself for falling into his trap. This accursed wilderness. This place without pity. This vengeful, lonely, savage place. Why had I come here? Who needed me? I couldn't open my mouth without the whole rotten panoply of emotion spilling out: disappointment, fear, anxiety, guilt, anger, obligation. Why was I so greedy, so insatiable? Why did I think everything was possible? Everything coming to me?

I had presumed. Invaded his privacy. He wasn't my buck-toothed Boy Scout any more, he was a fully grown man whose hair was beginning to turn gray, and the relationship I was trying to preserve was an absurd anachronism, a parody of togetherness. I'd humiliated him. Naturally I could be nice, because I had the do-re-mi. How could he help but hate me for my superior power? For the mobility I had and he did not? But to have the gall, the cheek, the ingratitude to tell me so to my face!

"Flares!" I thought. "That's what I ought to do. Go out in the middle of the goddammed lake and fire off my fucking flares!"

6

Next morning Ben looked as if he hadn't slept very much. He looked soggy, like the ground, had failed to comb his hair or beard or to straighten out his collar. He was formal with me at breakfast and very solicitous. Would I prefer regular tea to Labrador, would I like it with brown sugar or with honey? With or without a dash of cinnamon? Did I think we ought to finish the first cheese first, or start on the second for variety? That was how we conducted wars in our family, avoiding one another's eyes, squinting at the table as we requested the passage of the saltcellar, knocking on one another's doors before entering, disappearing into work, or going for long, solitary walks. What a relief, I'd often thought, to throw a plate.

Ben made a point of using my stove handle every time he shifted the lid of the Airtight to add more wood, said it was an admirable tool, far too useful to be left hanging behind the stove, although he would be glad to drill a hole through the end of the handle and slip a leather thong through it, so that when he was not carrying it around with him it would be handy to the hot stove.

Of course he was sorry for what he'd said, and so was I, but I wasn't so ready to forgive and forget.

"Ben, do you think you could put up some kind of a post at the facility, something I could hang on to up there, so I won't fall through?"

"Sure, Mom, sure," he said, and addressed himself to the task at once, shaping a long length of lumber to a point, which he would insert into the ground next to the platform. Before I'd finished tidying up after breakfast, I heard him up in the woods pounding the post into the ground. "Bang, bang!" Pause. "Bang, bang, *bang!*" The post did not eliminate all the difficulties, or keep the rain off, but it did lend a certain stability to my morning ritual.

"All right," I said to myself grudgingly as I returned to the house over the Cryptic Creek bridge, "maybe I won't leave tomorrow. But I'm not going to spend another wet night in the Kiosk." For a high wind had blown the rain halfway across my mossy floor. If I came down with a cold and had to depend on Ben to take care of me . . .

"Ben, do you think you could possibly put up some kind of a door on the Kiosk?"

A door took a lot more doing than a post, and Ben was hard-pressed to come up with a sheet of plastic large enough to cover the big triangular opening. He could piece something together, perhaps, but all his uncut sheets were already in use protecting some extremely valuable timber from the rain. He took me a short way up the hill from the house to display his prime treasure, a hoard of thirty-foot lengths of Douglas fir, split straight and clean by means of wedges and worth a small fortune, if he could ever find a way to get them out to market.

I could see he thought it was self-indulgent of me to want a door. What it came down to in his mind was taking care of the Douglas fir or making friends, again, with me. "Now the shoe is on the other foot!" I thought. "See what happens the minute you accumulate a little surplus? You face the typical middle-class dilemma: Property Rights versus Human Rights."

In the end, he stripped the plastic off the Douglas fir and lugged it up the hill to the Kiosk. That was how we always made up in our family. By doing a job.

I offered to help him measure up a frame to match the doorway, but I only got in his way. So I stood nearby, with the rain pouring in a steady trickle down the brim of my hat, and admired the dispatch with which he set about the job. "I'll hinge it on one side. You'll have to lift it off the ground to close it. There'll be some play in the hinges. It'll be heavy, but maybe if you leave it ajar about a foot . . ."

He'd already cut the three lengths of wood to size, was kneeling on the ground lashing the first to the second with a heavy cord when I saw him sniff, lift his head, jump to his feet, and run up the hill behind the Kiosk, as if he'd smelled something on the wind. I saw him look at the ground, then heard him shout, "Hey! Here's a door! I made it when I built the Kiosk!"

Indeed, there was a sturdy plastic door leaning up against a tree. I was so pleased he'd found it, so glad he didn't have to risk ruining his wood on account of me that I forgot to ask what made him run up the hill in the first place. If he'd actually forgotten that he already had a door, he must have been awfully upset by the tension between us. "I really do appreciate it, Ben," I said. "I felt bad about your using your plastic."

"Oh, that's okay, Mom," he said, suddenly gay. "The only thing that bothered me was how you could possibly sleep, all cooped up like that!"

While Ben was displaying his capital accumulation, he showed me the deer hide he was curing in the shed and a shriveled membrane, the lining of the deer's stomach or something, which he was saving to use as parchment. He kept it in a long, flat wooden box; when he opened it, I saw that this was where he kept his rifle. I wondered how he looked, what sort of an expression was on his face, when he pointed the muzzle at the deer and pulled the trigger. I thought of the red blast of fire, of the bleeding wound, and the velvet eyes losing their luster as the life poured out through the bullet hole. "It's either her life or mine," he must have said to himself when he brought the deer's breast into concordance with his rifle. I couldn't bring myself to ask if he skinned and cut it up on the spot, or if he brought it home with him and had some secret abbatoir in which he did the butchering. I recalled Ben lying on the carpet in the living room, caressing our old dog Juno, remembered how he'd brought me a bird with a broken wing, begging me to take it to the vet; how he'd carried a fish home in a canvas bag and later taken it back to the pond because he only wanted me to see that he'd caught it, and how it made him feel bad for the fish to die, just for that.

The venison in the refrigerator was ripening, for it was over two weeks since he'd shot and dressed the deer. When I opened the door, the smell of game overpowered the smell of cheeses and the tart, sweet odor of the quarter of pineapple we'd saved from our first lavish feast.

"I think I'll pickle some of the venison now, and bake the rest," Ben said. He packed a solid chunk of meat into a cast-iron cauldron and cut the remaining meat into inch-square cubes, dropped them into a clean glass jar, added white wine, onions, and pickling spices, and shook the mixture vigorously. "Good for another two weeks, at least," he said.

While he built a slow-burning fire in the Airtight, using alder wood and adjusting the air hole at the bottom to admit as little oxygen as possible, he explained how the human body was an energy-processor, that its fuel consumption was much like the Airtight's. Some parts of the deer were more perishable than others. You always ate the heart and liver right away, not only because they didn't keep but because they were the most nutritious, the most digestible, gave you the fastest shot of energy. "Which is an awfully good thing, you know, because you'd never shoot a spring deer unless your own energy was pretty low. In fact, it's against the law, which is why I keep the hide hidden. Just in case. Once your batteries are recharged, and the body's crisis is overcome, you can take your time about eating the muscles. Even after you've finished the baked and pickled meat, you still have the jerky. Dried, deer meat's good for months.

"You've always got to gear your activity to the available food supply," he continued. "In winter, when your intake is low-energy starch, you only undertake low-energy projects. Reading, small repairs, details of carving. You feel sluggish, you've got to feel sluggish, reduce your activities to a minimum, like a bear hibernating . . ."

"What an incredible waste of time! How can you

throw away a whole winter, walking around half-asleep?"

"Why, what difference does it make?" Ben said defensively. "I don't have anything better to do. I read the dictionary through five times last winter."

The rift between us had barely closed, so I shifted tack. "But didn't it take a lot of energy to shoot the deer?"

"Sure did," he said, looking pleased with himself. "A couple of nights earlier a deer charged right through the camp with a wolf behind it. I heard it jumping into the lake, knew it was going to swim out to that first little island. The wolf was howling on the shore, but I jumped out of bed, got my rifle and flashlight, and took the skiff over to the island. You wouldn't think such a big animal could hide on such a tiny island, would you? Well, when I finally found it, it jumped off the high rock, back into the water. I followed it around the lake for hours, wouldn't let it land, but in the end it outlasted me. It was dawn when I got back home, empty-handed. Two nights later, I bagged this one on the road to Gilly's."

We walked down to the little beach together, taking our fragile peace with us. The wind had shifted to southeast. Ragged clouds made purple patches on the ruffled lake and tore themselves to tatters as they raced across the sky. I thought of laundry flapping on a line, of Monday morning innocence, of fresh starts after murky weekends. "Got anything I can wash, Ben?"

"I washed everything I own before you got here," he said. But there was a green plastic bucket standing in the long grass, and Ben caught me looking at a pair of gray underpants lying under an inch of water on the bottom. "Show me how you do it, Ben. I feel like washing."

He sighed indulgently, gathered a black rubber plunger and a flat flask of detergent from nearby. "Generally speaking," he said, "I let things soak for about ten days. Work the plunger up and down whenever I pass by. When things get to the decisive stage, I add detergent and give it a workout. You pour the soapy water off into the grass, on account of the tadpoles. Then you slosh the clothes around in the lake."

"Beats hitting with a rock," I said. And gave it a go with my own underwear and a couple of pairs of Ben's socks that were lying in the grass, finding, as I always have, a large measure of tranquility in a good scrub.

I made a crisp salad out of apples and celery and walnuts for lunch, cementing our goodwill. "Just like downtown," Ben said, munching happily. He told me he'd been thinking about planting a garden near the shore, that he might put the seeds in this afternoon. "There's a waxing moon," he said, "so the time is auspicious."

I'd never thought of Ben as a farmer, a raiser of crops. He hadn't the disposition for it, the humbleness of spirit. But it pleased me that he was planning ahead to augment his food supply. One of these days he might even reinvent the wheel.

We were walking down the slope to the garden when Ben ran ahead of me, down to the shore, and shouted, "Hey! Buddhi's been here and left the canoe! We can go places now!"

Indeed, just beyond the hanging socks a large, battered aluminum canoe lay on the sandy strand where the open-eyed kayak used to be. "Did he just steal up while we were having lunch? How come he didn't come up to the house?"

"He doesn't much like to talk to people," Ben said. "He's really into meditation."

"Great!" I thought, "Just who Ben needs for a next-door neighbor. Another hermit." And gazed over the lake toward the fourth island rising from the flat surface of the water, wondering what sort of a person would chose to live on an island on a lake on an island in a strait. It was like the man on the label of the old Quaker Oats box who held a book with a picture of a man holding a book on which there was a man so small that you had to take his being there on faith.

"What's Buddy's last name?"

"Clement, I think. But his name's not Buddy. It's *Buddhi*. It means Ultimate Wisdom, Divine Intuition. When he got *satori* he decided to change his name to Buddhi."

I wondered if it was by divine intuition that Buddhi had thought to provide me and Ben with a means of transportation, but Ben said he'd asked him to trade boats with him, ". . . just in case you did come," he added.

"How did he know I was here?"

"Everybody knows you're here," Ben said. "They heard your plane come down."

Ben's garden was close to the delta of Cryptic Creek, where the soil was black and fertile and supported a lush growth of grass illuminated by tiny pink and white flowers. He'd staked out a patch of earth about twenty feet by twenty with a square of string, had already turned over the soil within it. Big, unbroken clods, with grass still growing out of them upside down. He chopped at the clods with a digging stick, like an Australian aborigine. A homemade rake leaned up against a tree. It resembled him, I could not say how, it just looked like something he would have made. It was long and strong and straightforward, with nails driven at regular intervals along the cross strip; but it was far too heavy, and the nails caught among the roots.

He marked out rows with sticks and string, more taken with the overall design of the garden than with soil-sifting. Then he tore open paper envelopes adorned with colorful promises of beets, onions, pole beans, peas, lettuce, Swiss chard, carrots. "This earth is so rich, anything will grow in it," he asserted as he poked the seeds into the ground with his fingers. Overhead a stand of alders tossed in the wind, casting dappled shadows over the garden.

"Ben, won't you have to cut down a few of these trees? It takes a lot of sunshine to grow vegetables."

"Yeah, probably. But I hate to take responsibility for cutting more than one or two. It might upset the natural balance of the creek mouth. And I'm not sure I can justify it. I'm not sure I'll ever harvest a crop."

I did not ask why not, because I could see for myself why not. Agriculture was not what he was talking about. What he meant was that he might not be here when things came up. What he meant was that a garden required a commitment of his time, a commitment which he was not prepared to make. I did not inquire what better things had he to do with his time, why it was too much to take the responsibility of a garden, why he would not permit himself to plant and tend, would not permit himself to harvest a crop. Any kind of a crop.

Yet, when all the seeds were in, he did fetch a power saw from the shed and cut down two large trees—making enough space to let the sun shine on his patch of dug-up earth, but not enough to open his digs to inquiry or observation from the lake. The saw made an awful noise, soiled the crisp spring air with the acrid odor of burning gasoline, but Ben said it was worth the noise and the stink. It would have taken him two days to do it by hand. "I'm not a purist, like some people, you see . . ."

I tried to help by carrying off the big, light branches of the alder's crown, hoisting them above my head, but their standing relations clutched at the fallen brethren as they passed, and the tension between them wrenched my shoulder. So I shifted jobs and carried one length of log at a time up the hill to the house.

The bark of alder is a pale blue green, like fine jade, and mottled like the bark of sycamore. Its cross-grained surface bleeds a brilliant orange sap which, Ben said, the Indians used for dye. Stacked in a neat pattern against the rise behind the house, the pale blue bark and the round, orange planes made a gorgeous backdrop for our comings and goings.

I'd already offered the only practical suggestion I could, but I knew something more was needed if Ben was to have a food supply out of that garden by midsummer.

"How's about a fertility rite, Ben?"

"Sure! Know any?"

"No, but we can make one up."

He seized a board in one hand and his planting stick in the other and began a strong jazz beat while I stomped up and down in front of the garden plot, interspersing howls with "Prop-a-gate! Prop-a-gate!" Then I took the drum and Ben danced, adding some very fancy footwork each time he came to the end of the string.

"The Four Directions: that's who we've got to talk to!" he said, and began by bowing low to the east.

"You! God of the place where the sun comes up. Source of all energy. Source of all goodness. When you mount the sky, shine your rays on this, my garden. Thank you, God of the East. Thank you very much." He bowed again, with his right hand pressed to his stomach and his left against his back, just as when he'd played Sir Lancelot in the fourth grade.

I did a bit of a riff on the drum, and he faced south.

"God of the South, I apologize for cutting down two of your trees. It's hard to be nice to a person who's done you injury, but I ask your forgiveness. I had to let in sunshine on my garden. Look with favor on my vegetables. I'd appreciate it, God of the South."

"Tah-dah!" I said on the drum.

"God of the West, from where the late light comes, home of the westerly which governs all movement on the lake, I thank you for whatever light you can spare. Thank you very much, God of the West."

And then he turned to face the dark wall of the forest. Suddenly he looked very small and puny. Fear clutched my heart, and I remembered the relentless cold of Canada, remembered the snow which blew straight down from the north pole over jagged, rasping mountains, drawing blood out of stones.

"I have little to say to you, God of the North, except to ask that you *know* that I have planted this garden here." He bowed very low, and his jaw was set.

I felt a sudden anxiety to interrupt that dangerous communication. "How about Earth Mother? You can't forget her. . . ."

"Jesus!" Ben exclaimed, horrified at his own negligence.

This time I did the talking for both of us. We made obeisance, once, twice, thrice.

"Goddess of the Earth in whom these seeds are planted, take them unto yourself and cause them to grow strong and bear fruit. Make these seeds into genuine Swiss chard and genuine beets and spinach and lettuce and onions. Use your great power on Ben's behalf, O Earth dear, for you are our mother. But I am Ben's mother. And it hurts me when he is hungry."

We lifted our arms toward the heavens. "May the words of my heart be acceptable . . . be acceptable . . ." goes the litany.

Ben rose first, "Listen, all you sky gods. We're just about to shut this show down. How's about you send us a sign that you've heard us?"

Before I could demur, the sun disappeared behind a cloud, a sharp wind rose on the lake, and there was a ping-ping-ping peppering the foliage.

"Hail! It's the sign!" cried Ben, dismayed.

The gods were imminent, their intention malicious. Ben had not done his homework properly and they were going to flunk him. There had to be something, some one correct response; it rose, bubbled up in my mind through layers upon layers of acquired knowledge.

I picked a pair of crystal pellets from the shining surface of a fresh green leaf, and handed one of them to Ben.

"Eat it!" I commanded, and popped the other one into my own mouth.

Before the ice had melted on my tongue, the sun came out, igniting a million pale green candles on a million evergreen branches. Out of the darkness and chaos, the fallible, botched-up world was about to begin all over again!

"A feast! We must have a feast of celebration!"

"Right! I'll go hunt up some mushrooms!"

"Nothing hallucinogenic?"

"Nothing hallucinogenic," he cried, dashing off into the woods.

7

While the sun sank in an extravaganza of celestial show-manship, we sat on neighboring stumps, digesting dinner. Ben, of course, was the first to notice a low thrumming on the lake. "That's Earl and Stukey coming back from Camp-bell River," he said. Moments later a frill of white water appeared near the southern shore of Tibbett Lake. The drone of a motorboat reached full volume, then diminished as the boat disappeared behind the first island.

Ben had mentioned Earl and Stukey in the next-to-last letter we'd received from him, around the end of March. They were independent loggers, harvesting the hundreds of windfalls floating on Tibbett Lake. "It was a shock and a lesson to me," he had written, "because up till now I thought of all that beautiful lumber as mine. At least, po-tentially mine. But I'm so glad to have somebody to talk to, I don't mind what they do." It was the first time he'd ever

admitted to loneliness. I had read the words like a sema-
phore, an SOS, and within the week I'd made a reservation
with the travel agency.

"Man, those guys are really *authorized,* " he said to me
now. "Got permits from Forestry, from Wildlife, from the
Company, plus a contract from the American tycoon who's
bought up all the land around Passmore Creek, where the
old flume is. It'll be good for the lake, clearing all that wood
out. The tannic acid in the bark poisons the bottom." Then,
in a scoffing voice, "That American thinks once they take
the stuff out he'll be able to go trout fishing in Passmore
Creek."

"Won't he?"

"Not when those guys get through with it!"

I asked Ben if I could see how Earl and Stukey worked.
I wouldn't have wanted to witness the felling of a forest.
It would be like visiting a war. But the operation at Passmore Creek sounded old-fashioned and ecological, up to a
point. Ben was glad to take me, for he wanted to have a
word with Earl and Stukey. While we were there he would
pick plantain for our dinner, provided the tide would be
out. He'd check it in the Tide Book.

It had not occurred to Ben, apparently, that I might
not know how to paddle a canoe. His instructions were
minimal. "Step firmly and squarely into the middle of the
bottom. Balance your beam on the forward thwart. Don't
wriggle. Always put the paddles in first." He did not criticize me when I dug the paddle straight down into the
shallows, pulled in the wrong direction, gave up after six
strokes. He managed the canoe from the stern, in spite of
my assistance.

It was wonderful, the way the world suddenly expanded out on the water; what a sense of freedom, of ease, of safety from lurking enemies infused my spirit. I could even identify a huge hawk hovering over the smallest of the islands.

Ben said there was a gull's nest out near the middle of the lake, with five beautiful olive green eggs in it. "Ah . . ." I said. "Five eggs. Just like me." And I was thrilled to be let in on such a secret hideout. A nest in a deadhead in the middle of a lake! But as we drew near, two enormous seagulls rose out of nowhere and commenced such a screaming that I plugged up my ears with my fingers. While one wheeled high overhead—the father, surely, taking the larger view—the mother swooped toward me in a Kamikaze dive, making straight for my eyes.

"Don't wave the oar around! You'll tip us over!" Ben cried as the canoe slid close enough for me to take a quick peep into the grassy nest. There were four eggs in the nest, not five. Lovely, large, olive green eggs. I pulled the hood of my jacket over my head in the nick of time, for mother gull dove again and again, determined to pluck out my eyes.

"They're the most hysterical damned birds!" Ben said as we glided out of range. His voice was heavy with disapproval.

But I understood the mother bird perfectly. Wasn't I just like her?

"What do you suppose happened to her fifth egg?" I asked.

Past the gull's nest, the water grew troubled and turbulent. Unlike the gentle ripples around Ben's sheltered harbor, waves mounted into yard-long hills and troughs and struck the metal bottom of the canoe with a loud "thunk!" The wind was behind us and drove us across to the southern shore before I realized how far away from home we'd been blown. The inlet was a narrowing of the lake, a place where low hills came close together and trees hung diagonally over the water, struggling for *lebensraum*. Hundreds of old, dead logs crowded the inlet. They were shore trees that had died by drowning seventy-five years ago when the level of Tibbett Lake was raised eight feet to provide momentum for the passage of timber out to sea through the flume at Passmore Creek. When the floating timber blocked our further passage, Ben tied the painter of the canoe to the roots of a deadfall shaped like an eagle with outstretched wings.

I followed him up a steep clay bank and through a thicket of shiny-leaved salal which tore at my jacket and snapped at my eyes. Again and again we had to climb above the roots of trees in order to pass between them, so crowded were they, so helter-skelter in their growth.

"Harry Fox hacked out this path," Ben said apologetically. "You can tell what a slob he was."

Suddenly Ben slid down a bank and I slid after him, finding myself standing on both feet in the middle of a logging operation.

A great expanse of floating logs covered the inlet, shore to shore, jamming up at the far end in a funnel-shaped declivity. On a raft nearby stood a blunt-nosed, mud-caked, yellow caterpillar tractor. And alone in the distance a skinny man with loose legs danced like a marionette from one twirling log to another, tipping a long pikestaff a little way up and then a little way down.

Ben walked in the general direction of the log jam, while the logger worked his way in the direction of the shore. If each of them continued in a straight line for forty paces, they would meet one another face to face. Neither allowed the other as much as a shifted eyeball, but their awareness of one another charged the hills. I followed Ben, waiting for him to present me to the logger so I could stride right up to him with a big smile and shake hands. I wanted him to know that Ben's mother had a strong, working hand.

The logger indicated his intention of stopping to talk by leaping over three twirling logs in a snappy pas de deux, fetching up cross-ankled just beside the yellow tractor. He had a sly, withered face, all tendons and no flesh. He was probably not more than thirty, but dried out, prematurely aged.

"Earl," Ben said, pronouncing his name deliberately, as if its use were propitiation to the logger, "how're ya doin'?"

Before he replied, Earl kicked a log with one foot and shot another into the vacated space with the other, altering the configuration of a dozen logs with a single forward thrust. It was a dazzling performance, and I knew that it was for me.

"Not too bad," he said at last. "Fin'lly got the skidder goin'." He nodded toward the tractor. A little farther down the edge of the lake, a large mound of mud and tangled roots blocked the passage to what appeared to be an open road. I guessed that the removal of the mound was the next step in clearing the way to drag the timber down to the shore. Passmore Creek lay at the border of the woods, a hundred yards or so down the inlet, too choked to be used, again, as a flume.

The two men stood opposite one another in silence, Earl planting his pike beside his feet and resting on it, and

Ben puffing on his pipe. I had never seen such caution, such circumspection. Did isolation and boredom magnify each human encounter, freight it with threat?

I stood aside, stared at the tips of my boots, awaiting my cue.

Ben said we were going down to the shore to pick plantain, that we had to catch the tide before it turned. He moved slowly off toward the break in the bank without looking around to see if I was following him.

I was outraged. Feeling the logger's appraising eyes on me, I caught up to Ben and hissed, "What the hell is the matter with you? Why didn't you introduce me to that man? Aren't women considered people up here?"

"And spoil all his fun? Why, your identity is worth a week of conversation between him and Stukey!"

"Well, okay. But I still think it was uncivilized not to introduce me."

We walked a hundred yards or so down an overgrown dirt road which roughly paralleled the creek.

At the end of the road we came out on a grassy slope of land with outcroppings of broad, flat rock. Beyond lay the sea. Salt air stirred the foliage and gulls dove under low-hanging clouds, complaining about a change in the weather. There was an oppressiveness and a feeling of suspense here, some intuition of danger that kept me from going any farther. I was unwilling to be a lone figure in so vast and open a landscape. I lacked the protective coloration. I did not speak the language, understand the rhythms. My timetable was out of sync. But I could not have admitted any of this to Ben. So I sat on a rock and watched while Ben crossed the mouth of the creek by running lightly across a log, then ambled down the verdant shore, studying the grass. "Do I know him?" I wondered as he knelt to pluck the plantain and put it into his woolen tuque. He seemed so utterly at home. "Have I ever known him?"

There was an extraordinary tranquility in his face when he returned to me with his cap full of greens. The plantain was fluted like a slit drinking straw, and rich, Ben boasted, in vitamin E.

Earl and another man, whom I took to be Stukey, were standing side by side when we returned. Stukey, who wore an undershirt, was much the older of the two. He was nearly bald and heavily muscled, with a beer belly and luxuriant gray sideburns. He wore a thick, gold wristwatch band, which he adjusted with a fat finger. In his other fingers he held a half-eaten sandwich of soft white bread and a slice of baloney, greenish gray around the rim.

"Come up f'r a cup of coffee, young feller?" Stukey said to Ben. His voice was big and he flashed me a gold-filled, insinuating smile. "Place don't look like much. Put it up in two hours. But it's home!"

Ben nodded yes, and stuffed the plantain from his cap into a big pocket in his jacket. "You goin' to *eat* that crap?" Earl asked. Close up, his eyes were pearly white and lashless, his complexion sallow beneath a deep tan.

"Lookit my uncle, puffin', climbin' up the hill!" he mocked the older man, bypassing him. Home was a prefabricated plywood box, about ten-by-ten and six feet high, jammed into a hillside crowded with trees. A small electric generator stood outside, connected to the interior by heavy coils of black wire. There was a large, green plastic bag with a tear in it, surrounded by garbage.

"Will ya look at that!" Stukey said, picking up an enameled pan in which tomato soup had recently been heated. It was covered with hundreds of tiny, black mouse turds. "I'll get them bas—— 'scuse me, ma'am, I'll get them little buggers tonight. We got fifty mousetraps laid inside."

Earl had preceded us into the house, crawling under a blanket nailed to the top of an opening in the plywood. He stuck his head from behind the blanket and said to Ben, "It's okay to come in now. I'll put up the coffee."

As I crawled in after Ben, Earl was scooping up an armful of "girlie" magazines from his cot. He shoved them hastily into a dark corner and covered them with a jacket. Stukey, rubbing his hands together to brush off the crumbs from his baloney sandwich, shoved a big pile of blankets and heavy jackets from the middle of his cot to the end, and with a gallant little bow invited me to sit down. Ben sat on the opposite bed. There was barely standing room inside for the two hosts.

It was quite dark with the blanket flap down. A little light came in through the only opening, a small, square hole in the wall behind a cast-iron wood stove. A Coleman lantern hung from the ceiling, casting more shadow than light. All the space not occupied by the two cots was filled with cardboard boxes of groceries: cans and packaged convenience foods. While Earl prepared instant coffee in an electric pot on a shelf near the blanket-door, Stukey leaned over me and turned on a radio, the announcer's voice bawling bargains in Campbell River, invading the crowded space with brand-name schlock. Then someone with a tin ear and a clothespin on his nose began to sob, "I neeeeeed you! I waaaaant you! Wahhgh! Wahhgh! Baby, Oh!"

Stukey sat down next to me, heavily. The cot had weak springs, and I was thigh-to-thigh with Stukey. When I tried to move over, I slid right down again, even closer than before. "Ay-ah!" Stukey said with a sharp intake of breath, "Strike comin' up the fifteenth of next month. Whole province'll be shut down, tightr'na clam. No tugs movin', nothin'. Got to move this stuff outta here fast!"

Ben nodded, puffed at his pipe.

"Haven't seen a dollar in three months! That skidder cost six thousand bucks. Six grand. We had a third guy in with us, but we bought 'im out. *Got* to get our hands on some cash, man!"

"Done any goose-hunting lately?" Ben inquired, picking up, I thought, on an earlier conversation.

"Nah, no time. Yeah, and that about you buildin' me a kayak, guess I'll have to put it off a while. . . . Fall, mebbe. Sure would be great havin' one o' them little buggers in a duck blind. . . ."

So! Ben had talked business with Stukey! Instantly, I felt more friendly toward the man and, when Earl handed me a cup of hot coffee, I smiled up at him with gratitude. Feeling I ought to say something to acknowledge their hospitality, I said, "Must be sort of lonesome for you up here."

Earl laughed dryly. "Oh, we got plenty to keep us busy. Play cribbage, bet on the hockey scores for drinks. . . . Why, last time Stukey paid off I tied one on for three days, down t' Courtenay. 'N it didn't cost me a cent!"

"Never you mind, Prince Charming," Stukey said, peering at Earl over the rim of his coffee cup. "I'll get you!"

Something, I realized, was crawling up my spine. It was not a mouse. It was too large and flat for a mouse. It was Stukey's hand.

I swallowed my coffee so fast I burned my mouth. Stukey's hand was exploring under my jacket.

"I'd be glad to help you fellows out, if you need an extra hand . . ." I heard Ben say.

"He's already *got* an extra hand!" I wanted to yell at Ben, who was, I realized, making a job application!

In one swift motion I set the coffee cup on the floor and bolted to my feet.

"Think we'd better be going?" I said to Ben and backed toward the hanging blanket.

Ben looked acutely embarrassed. As I was crawling out backwards, I heard him making circumspect departure comments, a lot of "ahhhs" and "well, uhhhs." I stood outside and heard Earl saying ". . . you ain't such a bad-lookin' kid. Y'oughta be able to do bettern' *that*. Why, that dame's old enough to be your *mother!*"

"She *is* my mother," Ben said.

"Hey, Stukey! Ya hear that?" cried Earl.

"Shhh—h!" Stukey hissed. "——— the hell'sa matter with you?"

Earl poked his head out from behind the blanket, his jaw open like a broken hinge.

"Well, I'll be go to hell!" he declared.

But Stukey pushed past him, lumbering out of the shack, following Ben.

"So long, ma'am," he said, smiling broadly and touching his gold-ringed fingers to his forehead. ". . . be seein' ya. Soon!"

"Do you think they'll give you a job?" I asked Ben as we scrambled down the hill.

"No," he said. "They're desperate, but they're not *that* desperate." I did not inquire whether Ben had changed his mind since I'd come and was now willing to make a concession to bourgeois ideology by working for cash.

"What did you jump up like that for?" Ben asked mildly as we climbed back into the canoe.

"That son of a bitch gave me a quick feel!" I muttered. "Stop laughing! I don't see what's so funny about it!"

A west wind was waiting for us at the end of the inlet; gusting down the mountainsides, whipping up the surface of Tibbett Lake like a beater in a bowl. The water was gray now, and roiling with froth. Though we paddled like fury, the wind caught the canoe on the flat. It struck against the top of the swells like a hammer. "Stop paddling!" Ben called. "We'll let her drift over to Buddhi's Island and then take her around the inland passage."

I drew in my paddle and lifted my face to the cold, clean rain. How glorious it was to be out in the open, to be free of that shoddy place, to be borne down the lake by natural forces, secure in the knowledge that Ben was in charge.

"Isn't this marvelous!" I cried over the whistling wind.

"Sure is, Mom! But please don't turn around again. You'll tip over the canoe."

When we neared the little island, Ben told me to paddle as hard as I could. We slipped out of the wind and into a tiny harbor, another log-strewn inlet, guarded by the exposed root of a snag shaped like a flying pterodactyl. Ben uttered a cry like a raven's, but there was no response except the chucking of the lake, the laughter of a loon.

"Think he's sleeping?" I whispered.

"Reciting *sutras*, more likely," Ben said, uttering the raven cry again.

"Are you sure he's here?"

"Yup. The kayak's here." He nodded toward the little

craft pulled up on the shore, its open eye lidded by the low-hanging yellow fronds of a big cedar.

"Maybe he thinks it's a bird? You sound exactly like a bird to me!"

"No. He must be busy. Let's go . . ." he said, and maneuvered deftly out of the maze of logs and onto the lake. It was only a moment before we reached the island's leeward side, and from there it was an easy passage home.

8

The door on the Kiosk made a big difference. Not that a plastic door would keep anyone out who wanted to get in; a plastic door was a pure illusion. On the other hand, illusions were not to be scorned. Thus enclosed, I slept soundly that night, for the first time.

It rained again next morning and the big trees creaked as they swayed, like the working of a wooden ship. Every time he went in or out of the house, Ben left the door open behind him, and every time he left the door open, I closed it. That is to say, I attempted to close it, because it was only a loose triangle of plastic with a round of wood, about two inches thick, nailed to the bottom to weigh it down. The only way to keep all the wind out was to shove the big armchair against it. "I'm going to put up a hook so I can fasten the door, Ben," I said.

"I hate closed doors," he said. "I like to be able to get

94

out in a second, if I have to."

"How like his father," I thought, for Hal always slept with his feet sticking out of the blanket, to be ready to fight off invaders.

Nevertheless, Ben did put a metal hook, actually a bent nail, on the vertical doorpost, and made another one to correspond with it on the flap. Snug against the wind, the little house felt cozy. Ben dug an old pair of felt boots out of his treasure chest and sat me beside the Airtight with a book. When Gussie hopped across the floor, I did not jump out of my chair. I said "Hi, Gussie," and reminded her not to knock over the tea kettle.

Variations of venison and vegetables rolled around in my mind. The plantain tasted good, but boiled down it came to a forkful-and-a-half for each of us. I longed for something that would stick to my ribs. Potatoes tonight, I decided, and tried not to think about crusty loaves of freshly baked bread.

I was grating carrots for a side dish of raisins, apples, and carrots when I glanced through the window facing the lake. The sun had come out a little while before and the trees sparkled with raindrops. Something moved, and it was not Ben. It was a man, and he was coming toward the house, taking a few steps, pausing to look around, taking a few more steps.

"Stukey!" I thought, and dropped the knife on the counter. What should I say to him? Should I just open the front door, put on my cool suburban face, and say, "Yes?" as if he were from United Parcel?

But it was not Stukey. It was a wild-haired young man in a raggedy-drooping rain cape, wearing pants that came down only as far as his knees. Save where rivulets of water made pale, crooked trails into his bushy beard, his face was as grimy as if he'd been rolling around in dust.

"I'm Buddhi," he whispered as I pushed my way out the front door flap. He smiled beatifically, as if being Buddhi was a universal joke, waved his hands in gestures of diffidence, meekness of spirit, and general helplessness, and nodded his head again and again, as if having started it bobbing, he did not know how to make it stop.

"I'm Ben's mother," I said. He blushed furiously, the rivulets on his skin turning deep pink. "I know," he said with visible effort.

"Ben's around here somewhere. I'm just fixing dinner. Will you join us?"

No, he would not eat with us, thank you, he had eaten just before he came. He folded his hands against his chest, tilted his head to the side to assure me he meant no offense, implied no criticism, did not wish me to feel badly at his rejection of my hospitality, and whispered that he was a vegetarian.

"We've got vegetables, too . . ."

"No," he said again, and kept a careful distance from me as he followed me indoors, taking Ben's high stool to the farthest possible corner of the house and sitting on the very edge. Even crowded into a corner he took up considerable space, for he was built like a football player. The hair on his face and beard stood out, as though electrified. His feet were thrust into rubber, dime-store sandals. Old dirt was caked between his toes and on his hands.

Ben bumped into Buddhi's knees, coming in the back door with his cap full of mushrooms. They greeted one another in hushed voices, as if each of them was afraid to wake the other one up. There was no small talk, except that

Ben thanked Buddhi for the loan of the canoe and Buddhi replied that he liked the kayak better. Ben told Buddhi that he'd put in his garden two days ago, and described our fertility rite and the hail which resulted from it. Buddhi nodded solemnly, as if to say he was glad that everything was in proper order around here. It was eerie, preparing dinner and eating it in the presence of a nonparticipating visitor, but Buddhi would not share our food. Halfway through the meal, he said he'd brought along his *go* board and if Ben was not busy, perhaps they would have a short game after dinner.

By nightfall Buddhi had become a fixture in the corner. Ben brought his newest chair into the house and the two young men leaned toward one another over the checkered, wooden board. I turned the collar on one of Ben's old shirts. The Aladdin lamps said "Ahhhh!" Small creatures of the night stirred in the forest, and the only other sound in the house was the sound of a single hand, clapping.

"Tell me about that boy, Ben," I said to Ben next morning.

"He plays a terrific game of *go.* "

"Oh, come on, Ben, don't be like that. Is he here on account of the draft?"

"You want me to give you a case history? No, in fact he was in the submarine service in Vietnam. He and his best friend volunteered at the same time. He got into the antiwar movement over there, and when he got out he started organizing veterans against the war."

"You don't mean it, Ben. He's no political activist!"

"Well, he used to be. This friend of his was wounded, in a VA hospital in southern Illinois, supposed to be discharged in about a week. Buddhi looked him up, talked him into taking a weekend pass to go to a peace meeting up in Chicago. They were hitching when this truck pulled over. The friend got in, and the truck driver pulled out a gun and shot him through the head. His good deed for the day. He shot a hippie. Nearly drove Buddhi out of his skull."

"My God, Ben! Oh, my God!"

"He comes and goes, never stays around more than a month or so at a time. People up here think he's a little crazy because he doesn't talk much, but he's all right. He's strong as an ox. Last time he came, he carried two hundred pounds of food with him, took it across the strait in the canoe, did the whole portage all by himself . . ." He looked up at me. "Christ, Mom, what do you look so depressed for? It's not your fault. Buddhi's all right now. He's fine. He's happy. He's really into Zen."

"Listen," he said, leaning forward as if I were the child and he the parent. "I'll tell you what. There's going to be a clam tide tomorrow morning. I looked it up this afternoon in the Tide Book. How about tomorrow, you and me'll go back to Tibbett Bay and collect some clams? It's time to vary our diet with shellfish."

I rose and took his round face in my hands, grateful for his concern. "Sure, Ben," I said. "Sure. That will be great fun."

Indeed, it was a lovely day. Clear sky, and the warmest it had been since I'd come to Proctor's Island. The wind was blowing from the southeast, just strong enough to make an easy paddle of the run to the south shore. We packed a lunch of apples and raisins and walnuts, and took along a thermos full of hot tea, for the coffee was all used up by now. I carried the lunch in a backpack and Ben carried his long-handled shovel, with a collapsible orange bucket hanging from the end like a Japanese lantern.

We tied up at the end of an old logging road, about half a mile this side of Earl and Stukey's. It came out pretty close to the plantain patch, Ben said, and it would be easier going than the salal-infested trail which only an idiot like Harry Fox would call a path. We had to ford a wide stream, a tributary of Passmore Creek. Since I was wearing rubber boots, I would probably have no trouble getting across.

There were deer tracks on the road, and the tracks of wolves. Ben said they were everywhere. It didn't mean anything except that the animals came down to drink at the stream. The tracks meant something to me, though, and because I kept my eyes glued to the ground, I missed seeing an eagle dropping into a nest on a barren snag less than thirty feet away. Long before we reached it, I heard the stream, for a steep waterfall intersected the road. Water rushed around a sharp bend, boiling with energy before it tumbled, slick as glass, over the rock. "You ought to see the salmon jump this fall!" Ben shouted above the uproar. "Silver flashes! Like magic!" He smiled as I had not seen him smile since I came.

I could have gotten drunk on the beauty of the falls myself; could have sat for half a day watching for a salmon. Below, where the white water crashed, a tiny dipper bird darted in and out of the stream, stiff-legged and plucky, snatching sustenance from the torrent.

Crossing the water was a tricky maneuver. Ben found a stout staff on the floor of the forest and I used it like a pole vaulter to get from one side to the other. Acknowledging his praise with a little bow, I said, "It's a good thing I came this year. In another couple of years I won't be able to leap around like that any more."

We came out on the shore side a few yards away from the plantain patch. If Ben did not assure me that we'd been here only two days ago, I would not have believed it. The sky was in mint condition, a polished, cerulean blue. Sunshine danced on the distant waters of the strait, a ribbon of diamonds strewn at the feet of hazy purple hills. Yards from the grassy margin under our feet, yesterday's bay had become a broad corridor of flat, wet sand, veined with pebbled, meandering streams, and ending in a long island, with sunlight pouring through the trees.

A boom of logs lay across the flat, ending on the grassy slope, the last of them chained to a granite boulder. "Those jerks!" Ben muttered, "Dumping logs all over the plantain!"

The grinding of heavy machinery floated over the island from the farther side, and from back in the woods beyond the mouth of Passmore Creek the skidder grunted and snorted. Ben hurried, crossing the sand, hopping over the shallow, freshwater streams as if he wanted to get out of sight as quickly as possible; but I dawdled, captivated by the colored stones and the brilliant algae, orange and green, moving sinuously in the sparkling waters.

Where the island's hump concealed us well from the masters of progress and technology, Ben set down the bucket on the sand and surveyed the field. It was exactly a month since he'd been here last, yet there were still small mounds of mud dotting the flat where he had dug before.

"There are forty-pound clams down there," he said. "If you hit them with a shovel, they bite." And to prove to me that he was not joking, he cut across a smooth airhole two inches in diameter, with his spade. "Did you dig one up?" I wondered. "Did you ever see a forty-pound clam?"

"No," he said, "my energy ran out before I got that far. But they're down there all right."

Today we were after smaller game, quahogs which appeared on an average of six to every shovelful of overturned mud. Ben did the digging, and I poked around with my fingers, extricating the clams. It was hard work, stooping down and clumping around in boots that sank inches into the sand at every step. We peeled off our jackets and then our sweaters, and by the time the orange bucket was nearly full we were both in shirt sleeves, sweating. When the sun reached its zenith, Ben called a halt, draped the jackets over the handle of the spade, and stuck it upright in the sand, making a spot of shade for the bucket of clams. We repaired to the island's rocks to eat our lunch.

Across the strait, small steamers plied the waters, marking the passage of time. Ben spotted a mink scurrying along a ledge, pointed out a heron fishing on one leg near the western shore of Tibbett Bay. He told me about crossing Dyer Strait one night in a borrowed skiff, and of being surrounded by a pod of killer whales. "They're misnamed," he assured me. "They're really gentle animals. They were just playing." He offered me a string of jerky, for energy, insisting that if I chewed it long enough I would get some flavor out of it. I chewed and chewed, but it still tasted like a rubber band.

It was idyllic, watching the clams squirting random fountains out of the sand flats. There was a sense of suspension in the moment, of interstice, of change. Something good and fundamental and nourishing was laid bare when the tide was out, something was uncovered and accessible which at other times lay under water, concealed, beyond reach. I framed the picture in my mind, committing each detail to memory. Suppose, I asked myself, suppose I failed? Suppose, after my visit, my relationship with Ben curled up and faded like a yellowing photograph. I would still have this moment. I would always have this sunshine, these trees, this open sky, this bucket of clams we had dug, together, out of the wet, yielding earth. This boy beside me was my son. It was I who had given him life, released him from nonbeing into experience, into suffering, into consciousness. He was a product of my passion and of his father's, and perhaps in his irrationalities, in the nobility of his private obsessions, he bore the stigmata of that passion. I was his mother. He was my son. Nothing could alter that fact. It was as legitimate in its way as the salmon's silver leap, the gull's cry, or the burrowing deep of the forty-pound clam.

I was so happy, I hurt.

We washed the clams off carefully in a salt water channel. Ben knew the salt water from the fresh without tasting to see which was which. It was important to wash them here because they'd have died in Cryptic Creek, and their chemistry would have polluted the stream. Even with the sand washed off, the bucket of clams was still too heavy for me to lift, but Ben swung it up to the end of his shovel as if it had no weight at all. This time when he hurried across the sandflat, I splashed right after him, for each little wave and ripple rolling in from the strait reclaimed another few inches of sand.

The tide was coming in again, fast.

Within an hour of our homecoming, Ben steamed half the bucket's contents and hung the rest over the shovel handle in the deep, dark pool in Cryptic Creek. Chilled, they would keep for another two days, at least. We melted a good-sized chunk of butter in a saucepan, added the juice of a lemon, and made a large dent in the mayo jar to lace the last of the fresh cabbage into cole slaw.

"If we only had some flour, I'd have made hot biscuits," Ben said. "We'll go over to Gilly's in a day or two."

I'd have given my arm for a hunk of bread, but I said to Ben, "It doesn't matter. We're living like kings. Kings!"

We ate clams until we were nearly comatose. Ben dumped the shells into his nonsoluble, nonbiodegradeable, noncomposting garbage pit. I staggered up to the Kiosk and slept all afternoon. The sun was going down when I awoke, and I wondered what time it was. The heirloom watch said quarter to eleven. I hadn't wound it or worn it for days. It was much easier than I ever thought, to do nothing in particular, as long as Ben was in the immediate vicinity. I had no need to talk, but I did have need of his presence. When he wasn't within hailing distance, the forest closed in on my spirits, and I curled up on the inside like a worm. Still, I required the appearance of doing something, so I took a book and went down to the beach; but the printed words became a pale gray blur that offered less competition for my attention than the green lichen on a boulder near the water.

I was delighted when I spotted the kayak moving toward the little harbor. The Buddhi in it was quite a different-looking Buddhi than the befuddled incompetent who had visited us the day before. His eyes were bright, his face and hands and feet were scrubbed, his hair was combed and tied with a headband, he looked absolutely civilized. "The power of the female!" I thought, congratulating myself.

"Hello!" he called out in a strong, cheery voice. He had

a nice way of pronouncing his ls. Quite delicate and refined. And he did not hurry past me to get to Ben; he pulled the kayak up onto the sand and hoisted himself up onto the long log, with his feet dangling down, to talk to me.

"Tell me about yourself, Buddhi. Where are you from?"

He laughed at my standard opening and gave me standard answers—name, rank and serial number, as on an application form or a curriculum vita—which were what I wanted, instead of a lot of hocus-pocus. I would astonish Ben with the data, later on. I knew he would wonder, "How did you get all that information?" And that I would reply, "By asking."

Buddhi's family lived in Milwaukee. His father was in the furniture business, and his mother was, well, she was his mother. When he was still called Clem, he'd gone to the University of Michigan, majored in anthropology, got halfway through graduate school but left to join a Zen community. "Ben tells me you're into the Tao," he said, as if it were marvelous that a person of my age should still be capable of thought. "Far *out!*"

"Ben exaggerates. I've only read the prefaces. I've never read the *I Ching.*"

"I used to be a Marxist," he said, wriggling his strong, crooked toes, "but the Marxists have no feeling for self-development. For them, all evil is on the outside. On the other hand, the mystics are awfully reactionary. It's tough to figure out what's right."

He was not putting me on, he was in dead earnest. If he'd reached those conclusions through meditation, there was more to sitting still than I'd ever thought. "What a neat formulation!" I said in genuine admiration. He blushed and said softly that it wasn't an original idea. At least, not entirely. It was simply his personal experience. He told me about an ecology group he'd worked with, which took the position that the killing of whales was inhuman. "But who is more inhuman than mankind?"

The longer he talked, the higher I got, not only because his thought was, itself, stimulating and cogent, but because he was an educational resource for Ben. He even agreed to join us for a couple of boiled potatoes. By tacit agreement, neither Ben nor I mentioned clams.

I sat back and listened while they discussed the moving out of the cedar shakes and the coming meeting, expecting their talk to be interlarded with denunciations of the multinational monster that was eating up the forests. But no. Their passion was all directed against "Fat City." Any Fat City. The superorganization of urban life, its corruption, constraint, unhealthiness. Cities created robots, deprived people of spontaneity, freedom; they bred ignorance, apathy, cowardice.

"Balls!" I thought. "Have they ever ridden a New York subway? Talk about courage, cunning, and endurance!"

I managed to keep quiet until Buddhi attacked the Sierra Club, which opposed all human residence in the remaining wild lands of North America. "I need a place to live, the woods are here, why don't I have a right to live here?" Buddhi inquired rhetorically.

"Yeah, the Sierra Club's just a bunch of sentimental city people," Ben agreed.

"Listen here, you guys," I interrupted, never suspecting how far I was going to go, "if everybody did what you're doing, the place would be loaded with fried potato stands. The only reason it works is that there are so few of you here."

"People don't *have* to spoil a place by living in it, Mom," Ben said. "They can be taught to take care of the forest. Who cares more about a place than the people who depend on it for a livelihood? If all the decisions are left to those chairwarmers in Vancouver, they're bound to mess things up because they don't know what's going on. All they care about is their stupid paychecks."

"But how can you control how people live? What about guys like Earl and Stukey?"

"Make rules," Buddhi said, marvelously unconscious of the irony. "People can keep an eye on one another."

This selfless Buddhist had become a Jeffersonian populist while eating boiled potatoes. How profoundly American both of them were, how middle-class, taking the extravagant promise of their country at face value, converting "I want" into "I have a right to," just like the most avaricious of our fellow countrymen! Neither of them took the exiled Indian population into account in their debate over the right to the land.

"Buddhi," I said, "Who keeps an eye on *you?* Besides, as soon as you've got keeping-an-eye-on, you've got cops, regulations, courts; in short, all the so-called evils of the city. It really bugs me, the way you guys put the city down. Don't you realize that every single idea in your heads came out of cities? Books aren't written by people sitting around studying their navels. Books are written by people who want to convince other people of something. Ideas are generated out of differences of opinion, out of the need to have a common understanding with people who differ with you.

If you didn't have cities, everybody would only know as much as had happened in their own life, in their own tribe. If you really lived in a primitive society and dared to question the rituals, you'd be stoned to death. The *only* place people can be free is in a complex society. . . .

"And furthermore, don't knock the Sierra Club. It's going to take a thousand years to undo all the damage that's been done around here. They ought to shut the whole place down, if you ask me. . . ."

I hadn't meant to say it aloud, but it was exactly how I felt. I could see that Ben was upset.

"You talk about these woods as if they were sacred," Buddhi objected. "There's nothing sacred about them. They're second growth!"

"Come on, Buddhi! And if they were virgin timber, they *would* be sacred? Listen, Buddhi, if the woods around Nootka Creek are not sacred, there is nothing sacred in the whole world."

Ben got up to get more firewood. "I'm sorry, Ben," I said, "I didn't mean to mount a soapbox."

"That's all right," he said, forcing a smile, "you have a right to your own opinions. It's just that I don't agree with a single word you've said. But you have the right to say what you think. Why not? That's what this place is for, isn't it?"

Buddhi said, "I like it when she talks. It's great!"

I insisted on washing the dishes, chiefly because my hands were cold and I liked the feeling of warm, soapy water. While Buddhi and I continued our conversation, I reached for the thermos we'd taken on the clamming expedition, to rinse it, because the stem of a leaf stuck out of the top. Thrusting a couple of fingers down the neck, the object

I pulled out turned out to be, instead, a drowned mouse. I yelped so loudly that Ben dashed through the door flap, his eyes black with alarm. "What . . . ?"

Buddhi picked up the dishpan, carried it outdoors, and poured the water off onto the ground. Crouching low, he brushed the soap bubbles from the mouse's tiny nostrils, freed its tiny, gaping mouth of soap. "It may still be alive," he whispered.

Ben stood over him with folded arms, watching, but the wet ball of fur did not move. He stooped, picked the mouse up by the tail, and with a wide gesture flung it into the woods behind the house.

"Either it's gonna live or it's gonna die," he said sternly. "You can't afford to be sentimental about mice."

9

I could have kicked myself. I had planned to save it for the very last, waiting for our final farewell to say, "Well, Ben, now that I've been here, I'm more convinced than ever that you ought to pack it in and come back home." But I'd lost control of myself. In the heat of the argument I'd spilled the beans, cut the ground from beneath the remainder of my visit. There was nothing Ben could do now, nothing he could show me that would transcend my blanket disapproval, contradict my flawless logic, compete with my rhetoric.

Of course I wanted the Company to throw Ben out. The only reason they hadn't done so already was that Ben and Buddhi and the rest of them were not worth the cost of prosecution. If they had been Indians, if they had had the traditions, the rituals, the ancestral claims, they might have constituted a threat; if not in the present, then in the future. Which was precisely why all the Indians were down in Campbell River, impaled on "civilization." Capitalists weren't stupid. They knew perfectly well who was living in their woods: middle-class intellectuals, transients without allies in the larger fabric of Canadian society. Would the pilot of Sea and Air Transport lift a finger to defend Ben's "rights"? They were outsiders, all of them, and they would be brushed away like flies at a feast the moment they got obstreperous.

The truth was that Ben and Buddhi were on an extended vacation from life. They'd escaped from Necessity. Found a free resort. A last resort. They weren't paying their dues, weren't giving back to society what society had given to them.

Ben had never had to face up to his government. The draft never reached his number, so he hadn't had to deal with it, go through the hearings, explain to the businessmen, the dentists, the troop captains of the Veterans of Foreign Wars, to the certified public accountants who comprised the local draft board, why he would not fight in Vietnam. We were all in Canada then, and when his name came up it was placed in a file cabinet in Washington reserved for Americans living abroad. No one in that file had ever been drafted. Ben had never had to define his position in relation to the draft, to weigh his options, discover the limits of his convictions, of his courage, by deciding: "If they tell me to do such and such, I will do so and so." I had no idea what his priorities might have been—if he'd have preferred jail to exile, or if he'd have become a conscientious objector—and neither did he.

It was time for him to face reality, to deal with the hard facts. It would do him a world of good. Let them come with their cardboard seaplanes and their stamped documents.

Let them call him down to the office and say, "See here, young man, this place doesn't belong to you, no matter how much you might like it here. You're not even a real Canadian, so clear out. On the double." If they said it, I would not have to. I could still be the good guy in the script.

Except that I'd already said it.

So what difference would it make if the Company put him out? The Forestry Service had already burned down one of his dwellings. If Proctor's Island became uninhabitable, legally, he'd move to the next island north and build himself a bigger house. He'd keep on going farther and farther north, beyond the range of cardboard seaplanes, so far that I would never find him again. The wilderness was inside of his head. And as for hard facts, what could be harder than the facts he inflicted upon himself?

I blundered, bleary-eyed, into the house next morning and felt bad vibes the moment I pushed through the door flap. We backed away from one another, preparing breakfast.

"Quite a change in Buddhi, eh?" I began. "Wouldn't have thought he was the same person . . ."

"Yeah. You're amazing. You have a talent for bringing people out."

"Nonsense, Ben. I just asked him to tell me about himself and he did. Do you know he was getting a master's from Michigan?"

"I never ask personal questions," he replied testily.

I laughed. "Don't be silly, Ben. He told you the most intimate experience of his life."

"That was *not* the most intimate experience of his life. It was merely the public explanation of his private religious conviction."

"Maybe. But I never expected him to be so . . . intelligent."

"What makes you think he's so intelligent? Just because he's been to college? Got the *Good Housekeeping* Seal of Approval for his brains?"

"Ben!"

"Well, you never talk to *me* like that. As a matter of fact, you hardly talk to me at all!"

"How can you say such a thing? Do you seriously think I don't respect your mind? My God, if I ever had a student in one of my classes with a mind like yours, I'd be delirious with joy! Why do you think I keep sending you books? Because I know you read them, which is more than most college students do. Why . . ."

"Yeah, and speaking of books, how come all the books you send me are about death?"

"About death?" I was thunderstruck. "What did I send you?"

"*Death in Venice. As I Lay Dying. Death in the Afternoon. A Death in the Family.* . . . I never read any of them, and I won't."

My hands trembled as I poured myself a cup of tea.

"Ben, I had no intention . . . I thought I was sending you the best of literature. Thomas Mann. Faulkner. Hemingway, Agee. The best writers of the twentieth century. I sure have been giving off the wrong signals. I just don't know how to convince you that I think you are an extraordinary person. That your courage, your resourcefulness . . . all that you understand about this place . . . who else could have done what you've done? Why, not since Robinson Crusoe . . ."

"Stop!" he cried fiercely. "Stop right now. Don't ever

say that about me again. It's romantic bullshit. It's what you've always done to me. Made me out to be some kind of a hero when I'm just a punk. When I failed algebra, you'd say, 'Never mind, I'll go up to the school and explain to them that you've got other aptitudes.' "

"That's not true! You failed algebra three times!"

"Never mind. It's not the point. You've always said to me, 'You're beautiful. You have a beautiful mind. You can be anything you want to be.' "

"But it's true! I still think it's true!"

"It's *not* true. It's a lie. You lied to me. I can't be anything I want. I'm not even a good shake splitter."

I sat down in the big chair, because I was not capable of standing up, held my head in my hands.

"Don't you see, Mom," Ben went on more gently now, but with urgency, "Don't you see that I never had to *do* anything? The clothes got handed down from Jesse, the food came in the back door—all I was ever required to do was eat it. Even now, you want to dress me up in a costume, make me play a role in some goddamned book. I'm *not* Robinson Crusoe, I'm me. Ben. I've got no job. I've got no money. I've got no company. I'm a failure. Why can't you face it?"

"It's only because you don't *want* a job. You don't *want* money. Why shouldn't you have these things? You're as good as anybody else, and a whole lot better than most."

"You're a romantic, Mom. I'm not. I'm not the least bit heroic. If I'd known what else to do, I'd have done it, plenty of times."

"But Ben, you could go to school, you could become . . ."

"There you go again. Suppose I want to be a failure.

Suppose there's nothing out there in Fat City I want? Suppose I have everything I do want, right here? Can't you allow that?"

It was a lot for him to ask—more, maybe, than I'd ever imagined I would have to give. I was strangling, trying to hold back the tears. ". . . Ben, I'm sorry if I've botched it, if my needs, if my ambitions got in your way. I only want you to know one thing: that no matter what you may think of yourself, I shall always . . . I shall always . . ."

What shall I always? There were no words to describe that tidal, engulfing feeling, that primal connection. It was fixed in me, built into my structure.

"Oh, Ben, I don't know why you . . . I just don't understand where you get the fortitude!"

He didn't reply at once, but when I looked at his face it had suddenly gone soft. His eyes were lustrous, brimming. "Don't you, Mom? Don't you, really?" he asked.

There was no place to go to get away from Ben, except down to the beach; that is where I went. If I were at home, I'd have taken to bed. Pulled the covers over my head and stayed there. My husband would have brought me hot tea and melted cheese sandwiches, played my favorite records, held me in his arms, knowing to the comma every thought in my head, every pain in my heart, and both of us would have pretended it was something I ate, because there is always a complicity of silence between best friends.

How perfectly Ben had cornered me. What a double-bind he had constructed. How cleverly he had managed his life, to defeat me. How could I ever have thought he was in need of my advice, of my protection, of my rescue?

Whose death was I thinking of when I sent him all those books? My own? I had a vivid image of my own mortality. Everyone catches a glimpse of it, one way or another. Yet, death is our best-kept secret. That was what I was whispering to him through the titles of those books: "It isn't going to last forever, my son. So make something of it while you have it."

And if it was his will that what he made of it was what he called a failure? What was failure, except a refusal to live? To take risks? To play the game?

I had to let him go, had to give up hope of prying him loose from his moorings, for the self he secreted was too fragile, too vulnerable for ordinary life. I had to take it on faith that buried deep in his being there was a core, a point at which all the vectors converged, that when the moment came when he would have to choose, some archaic memory of connectedness would energize the nerve; that he would not let the gift slip from his fingers because he believed it was of no consequence whether he survived or not.

I had to try to stop loving him, because I was the one he had come here to escape.

"How're ya doin'?" he asked, loping down to the beach with cedar shavings stuck all over his woolen jacket, clinging to his tuque.

"Fine. I was just collecting the laundry. It certainly travels. Everything's still soaking wet. Just like you said."

He stood near me but he did not look as if he intended to stay and talk.

"Ben, have you done any wood sculpture since you've been here?" I asked him, for he still hadn't taken his father's gifts out of the suitcase. Perhaps drawing was something he could only do in perfect privacy. Painting was more public. Our walls at home were covered with his wild abstractions and brilliant cityscapes, things he'd done during our last winter in Montreal, just before he left home. As if he were rehearsing a fantastic adventure in his mind before embarking on it in real life.

He rolled something out of the tall grass near the beach, a carving he'd begun during the winter. "A low-energy project. I could do it sitting down." It was a larger-than-life mask of a man with the mouth drawn down and the eyes tightly shut, locked in nightmare.

I thought of a Haida mask, a blue-painted face with round, hollow eyes and drawn lips that wailed "Wooooooo!" They were used to exorcise the cannibal spirit from the souls of young men, lost for long periods of time in the forest, who cut off an arm or a leg and ate themselves to keep alive.

Ben's carving lacked the stylization of the Haida mask. His was a highly personal statement, a portrait of a man who was dying of deprivation. I shuddered.

". . . I don't like it much, either," Ben said, "but I don't know how to finish it." And he rolled it back into the long grass.

"Do you have to finish it?"

I had gone too far.

"Say, why don't you take the canoe out and explore a little on your own. You can handle the canoe."

"Sure. Great idea. Exercise will limber me up."

My bones creaked as I climbed the hill to the Kiosk to fetch an extra sweater. I'd never handled a canoe alone. I was afraid to be in deep water by myself. But clearly, my company was a burden on Ben's spirits, just as his company was a burden on mine.

He held the prow of the canoe steady for me as I climbed in, and said, "Have a good look around. Don't hurry. You'll be all right." But as the canoe scraped off the sand into the water, he called after me, "Dad told me not to let you out of my sight." As if his father were standing behind his shoulder.

"When did he tell you that?"

"In a letter, a month before you got here . . ."

How long was the arm of the nuclear family! Ordinarily, Hal was not a letter-writing man.

I laughed across the widening water. "He had some nerve," I cried, "as if I weren't capable of taking care of myself!"

Tibbett Lake rolled away like a bolt of pale blue satin, scalloped at the selvage by pale blue mountains. Fifty miles west, the peaks of Vancouver Island framed the horizon in white lace, pretty as a post card. As I cleared the harbor, Madame Gull zoomed overhead and circled back to the deadhead to report to her mate that the enemy was proceeding in another direction. A kingfisher dropped from a high rock on the tiny island, making a conspicuous splash. I circled around, practicing my strokes while a pair of ducks flew along the shore in tandem, ruler-straight and bent on business. There was no romance in the bird society of British Columbia. None of the twitter, the embroidery, the extravagant promises of domestic bliss with which the birds back home deluded one another in the month of May.

It was a great relief to get away. As Ben's little harbor merged with the shoreline, my anguish over him diminished. I felt competent and free in the canoe, able to decide my own direction, capable of longer views. It shouldn't be impossible to give him up. My own life didn't depend on Ben. I had a fine, rich life.

Besides, nobody believed in mother-love any more.

Everybody understood it was a middle-class convention, a way of concealing property relationships by endowing them with emotion, an investment of one's ego in a product which bore the stamp of the manufacturer and reflected well or badly upon the source. Every literate person now knew that "caring" was a perversion of the ego-trip, a way of making one's self look good in one's own eyes; that all a mother really lost when she lost a child were the illusions and projections which she, herself, had lavished upon her or him. Wasn't self-deception the greatest discovery of the twentieth century?

Paddling peacefully around the second island, my view grew very long indeed. The whole issue could be reduced to a syllogism: "You belong to me. You cause me to suffer. My suffering must have value, since it hurts me so much. Therefore you have value. Conclusion: We value what we suffer for."

I regretted not having brought along a pencil and paper to write it down. If I'd only thought of it sooner, I could have mailed it to R.D. Laing. All I really had to do was recognize that it was actually self-love that motivated me, and guilt would do the rest.

The sunshine was a great soporific, beating down on my head, warming my back, making little rainbows on the drops of water splashing from the ends of my oars. I felt like throwing away the *New York Review of Books* in my brain, tossing it into the water, saying to hell with all of them, to hell with the *Saturday Review* and with *New York* magazine, to hell with the C.G. Jung Foundation and *Finnegan's Wake*. I'm sick and tired of the whole lot of you and I want you to get off my back. If self-deception was the greatest discovery of the twentieth century, self-analysis was its greatest indoor sport. But I was in the outdoors. I was further outdoors than any other person in North America.

There was a lot to look at on the lake. Close to the shore, a network of lily pads floated just beneath the surface, but there were no perfumed blooms to put me into a swoon. Even the air, here, was austere. No rank, rotting vegetation; just the sharp, clean smell of evergreens, like the burlap-covered balsam pillows rich relatives used to send as souvenirs of an Adirondack vacation.

A good half-mile down the lake from Ben's harbor, a large stand of drowned trees jutted out from the shore, rooted in what must have been a rise in the ground before the level of the lake was raised. I was paddling past, desultory and directionless, thinking to steer clear of it, for the trees looked grim and forbidding and barren as a prison yard. I thought I was moving away, but the prow of the canoe swiveled sharply and caught on the submerged roots of a huge deadfall. I tried to backpaddle, to push myself off, but the harder I worked, the more tenaciously the roots held on. Sweat began to trickle down my back. I feared to look up lest the ghostly malevolence of those trees reach down and grab me. Thrashing at the water with the paddle, I broke loose from the roots and lurched forward so violently that my head struck the outstretched limb of a fallen tree.

I pulled in the paddle and sat for a long time, holding my throbbing head. It was too ludicrous. What hurt me more than my head was my pride. Everybody had told me so. Be careful. Carry splints. Come back soon. Don't take foolish risks. Smile.

"Shit!" I thought. "Shit!"

And then I thought of the classic question posed in Philosophy 109: "If a tree falls in a forest and no one hears it, is there a noise?" That question had awakened more than one sleeping student to the ambiguous nature of reality. And a corollary: "If there is a joke and no one laughs, is it still funny?"

Of course it was funny. Wasn't I laughing?

For I had begun to laugh. In fact, I was laughing so hard I was shaking up the canoe. Because there was no one else here. No one but me, myself, and I. No one to deplore my lack of caution, no one to tie my brains into knots, no one to interpret my behavior, no dear little daughter to say "Come home soon, Mom"; no one to say "I told you so." I had permission to be a jackass. I could give myself permission, and no one would contradict me, interpret my behavior, criticize. No one was expecting me. I did not have to be on time for anything. I could stay here as long as I liked, trapped in my own folly. I was safe from the jaws of my loved ones!

Without making a plan, without devising a strategy, I laughed myself loose of the snag. The canoe eased from one small opening into another, following the current of the lake. Wherever I dipped my paddle, made a short thrust, little whirlpools dimpled the water's still surface, shifting the prow first in one direction and then in another. When the trees closed in, I withdrew the paddle and pushed against their gray, sun-warmed flanks with my bare palms until, ducking under the limbs at an oblique angle, I glided clear of the maze and out, free, on the open water.

The run across the inland passage to Buddhi's island was a five-minute affair, and I did not give a moment's thought to the water's depth. No one in the world would appreciate the significance of that episode as well as Buddhi. The whole center and purpose of Zen was to enable the driving and the driven to drop the ego, to let nature take its course, to do by not doing.

"Maybe I can get him to pronounce a few more ls," I thought, plunging the paddle below the silken surface of the lake, cutting across the water sharply and swiftly as a brand new scissors.

He was waiting for me, sitting in lotus position on a broad, flat rock, blinking into the noonday sun. Beside him on the rock lay a copy of the *I Ching*, a small, brass bell with a slim wand for striking it, a folded letter, and a United States Income Tax Form 1040.

"Consulting the *I Ching* to do your income tax return?" I said, climbing up the bank. His smile faded a little. For a fleeting moment he looked downcast. "It's more than a month overdue, but I guess the country won't go broke waiting. The interest on zero is still zero. I just haven't had the time to fill it out."

"How did the Feds get you on their list? Ever held a paying job?"

"Uh-huh. Worked on an archaeological dig down in Baja California last summer." He smiled at the memory. He had a bony, sloping forehead, high cheekbones, and small, blue eyes, deeply set.

"And will you teach, after you get your degree?"

"Probably not."

"Then what will you do?" Even as I asked the question, I heard myself functioning *in loco parentis*, my reflexes intact despite all my philosophical footwork.

Buddhi shrugged. "Nothing, probably. You know," he added confidentially, "it's practically impossible to starve in America."

"Why would you want to try? I mean, apart from a

spiritual exercise?"

"My parents don't understand it either," he said with a sad smile.

I settled my back against the trunk of a tree and told Buddhi about my adventure in the canoe, how the absurdity of it was the thing that liberated me, how I wished I really understood the Tao, could let go of the compulsion to accomplish, to alter, to analyze. I even understood that wanting a thing to happen was the best guarantee that it would not happen, because the wanting itself got in the way of the natural processes. I understood a little of it in theory, but it was very hard to change the habits of a lifetime. "My generation was raised on the slogan, 'Leave the world a little better place than you find it.'"

"That," he replied, "presupposes that a human being is capable of knowing what 'better' is. I'm not so sure about that. My only ambition is to have no ambition. It's very hard, but I work on it all the time."

It was easy to talk to Buddhi. I felt a freedom in our discourse, a permissiveness, as if his mind were an open door through which it was safe to pass. That there was no rebuke awaiting me, that he could view my struggles with interest and detachment.

So I went on, elaborating my thought.

"Maybe it's inevitable, in a highly individualistic society, for 'leaving the world a better place' to turn out in practice to mean 'a better place for *me.*' It does seem that the more creative and intelligent people are, the more cleverly and deviously they conceal their self-interest. I mean, Buddhi, you can go through all the big theories and see how they really were elaborate self-justifications. Freud was in love with his mother. Jung was coming to terms with his father's Christianity. Darwin was rationalizing British imperialism. And Wagner—sending all those heaving, passionate messages to somebody else's wife! It makes a person cynical to see that. But I guess the hardest part, for me, is to realize that it applies just as much to being a parent. You spend most of your life thinking you are doing things for your children's welfare, but when you look it straight in the eye you have to realize that you're really just doing it for yourself."

"You're a very honest person," Buddhi said.

"Well, that's a kind of a pose, too. A way of shoring up your battered self-respect."

"Why are you so hard on yourself?" he asked me. "Ben thinks you and his father are the greatest people in the world."

He'd caught me by surprise. I sobbed openly and without shame. "But I can't talk to Ben . . ."

In a little while Buddhi excused himself and retired to his ashram, hidden somewhere close in the woods. High overhead in the crown of a tree, a creature scurried along a branch, breaking off a leafy twig which spiraled slowly to the ground. Buddhi returned carrying two mugs of hot tea. When we'd finished it, he handed me his copy of the *I Ching*.

"I don't know how to do it, Buddhi. I haven't got any yarrow stalks. Not even pennies. I can't read a hexagram."

"It doesn't matter," he said. "Just open it up anywhere."

I took the book from his hands and it fell open to page 150. I read aloud:

Isolated through opposition————["That's Ben!"]
One sees one's companion as a pig covered with dirt
————["Is that what you and Ben call Fat City?"]

First one draws his bow against him,
Then one lays his bow aside.
He is not a robber, he will woo at the right time.
As one goes, rain falls;
Then good fortune comes.

"Oh, Buddhi, I shouldn't have come here, I should never have come. Don't you see, it's me that's the problem?"

"Read on," he ordered.

I wiped my eyes and nose with the back of my hand and read on.

Six in the fifth place means:
Remorse disappears.
The companion bites a way through the wrappings.
If one goes to him
How can it be a mistake?

"See?" he cried.

"But how do I get six in the fifth place? What do I have to do, to disappear the remorse?"

"You're already doing it," he said.

I guess I fell in love with Buddhi at that moment. I know I wanted to fling my arms around him, to make a pledge of life-long friendship. But I was eager, too, to get started on the biting-through-the-wrappings. Buddhi touched my arm and asked me not to leave, not quite yet. "Would you mind," he asked, "reading this letter before you go?"

The address at the top was Baja California. It was dated early in April. "Dear Father," it said. "Love, Steve and Linda." That was all.

He studied my face. "Do you understand what it means?"

"I . . . I think I do. Congratulations?"

His young face was transfigured with joy. "I have a child, too. I hope I can be as good a parent to my daughter as you are to Ben."

"But . . ."

"They are my best friends. They tried to have a baby for two years and couldn't. So they asked me. My daughter . . . my daughter is a month old. I'm going down to see her soon."

"Heaven help him! Heaven help them all!" I thought fervently. "The complications! His chromosomes!"

But I said, "I wish you all the best of health, the greatest joy, Buddhi . . ." And gave him a little hug, for becoming a father.

He returned my embrace shyly. "Yeah," he said, nodding his head as he had when we first met, "I'm into life, but I'm not into the nuclear family."

As I pulled the canoe away from the shelter of his island, he struck the little bell with the slender wand. Its vibrations spread in widening circles on the still, blue air and followed me like a benediction all the way home.

Only when I reached Ben's harbor did it occur to me that the reason he had not yet filled out Form 1040 might be that he did not know what to put down under "Number of Dependents."

10

Everything was right, finally, for the visit to Gilly.

The phase of the moon boded well for the journey. The wind was blowing in the right direction. It was getting to be time to talk about the shake sale and the meeting. While I was chatting on Buddhi's island, Ben had prepared a concentrate of clam chowder to add to his trading goods. "Simply add water and serve," he said with a commercial smile.

I required no elaborate justifications for making the trip. I was very fond of Gilly and curious to see how things stood between her and Ben. Perhaps there was a wrapping I might bite through. But more important, a visit to Gilly meant bread on the table and wool for Ben's sweater. I'd never undertaken a journey before with such crass ends in view, but my moral fiber was getting flabby.

Tibbett Lake was smooth as glass when we set out next

morning. Mist lay like a pink feather quilt tossed off by the slumbering mountains during the night, and cool exhalations of the forest followed us out of Ben's harbor. "Do you see up there, Mom, where it spells 'Ben's'?" he said, pointing toward the mountain behind his camp. "Not really," I replied. "Say!" he murmured to the back of my head, "The apostrophe just flew off!"

We moved from the mountain's purple shadow into midmorning sunshine, the little islands revolving like dark, green balls of glass as we passed. "Buddhi told me about his baby, Ben," I said as we neared his island.

"I knew he would when the moment was auspicious."

"Do you think he'd take some responsibility, in case the child had . . . well, special problems?"

"There can't be any problems. They took great precautions."

"Oh? Like what, for instance? If it's not too personal . . ."

"Timed it propitiously, on the best day of the year. Buddhi saved up his energy for months. There were lots of people there, chanting, meditating, getting all the vibes right."

Not such a bad idea, I thought. Being born is a risky business. An extra parent could come in handy. At least it was planned. Most people are born by accident. That was what the whole human race was: strictly the work of amateurs. As for chanting, in my time we did all our chanting out of Dr. Spock.

It took about half an hour to cross the lake. Ben had asked me to wear my watch so we could time the trip. "I think it's much faster with two people paddling," he said.

We tied the canoe to a huge old raft, skirted with

floating weeds. Dogwood flowered in the crevices, dog-wood being a bush in British Columbia and not a tree.
"Ben, I've got déja vu!"

"That's because you vu-ed it, déja," he replied. "This is where the pilot wanted to let you off last week. It's the official landing place for the interior of Proctor's Island."

The raft used to be the terminus of a logging operation that reached its height nearly forty years ago. Along the shore the evergreens were stunted, barely as high as my shoulder, forming a low scrub, stifled greenery struggling for air and space. A hundred yards or so up from the landing, we came upon a slash, a clear-cut. Hard-packed subsoil clung to black stumps, each with a torn and ragged edge where the bark hung on after the trunk was severed. It was hot and dry as a desert. Above rose a red granite rock face, a splitting off of a mountain that served now as a kind of monument to a collective destruction. I thought of newsreels of prisoners who dug their own graves at gunpoint, then toppled in, lucky to be dead when they fell. A dusty little snake wriggled out of the way of my heavy boot. So this was how the forest fared when the outward manifestation was hauled away and only the spirit of the trees remained!

"Nootka Creek is going to look like this if they get away with it," Ben said bitterly.

An old road wound through the slash, ending at an abandoned logging camp, weedy and rubble-strewn and bounded by a stand of young willows bordering a stream. I stopped to rest on the bank and doused my face with cold water. Among the grasses a tiny yellow flower, all spiky feelers and sticky seductions, was closing in on a tiny, black bug.

Ben roamed the Ruins, climbing mounds of earth encrusted with tractor treads and torn fenders, searching for parts for the bath he planned to build. Beside a row of wooden shacks with caved-in roofs and missing slats stood a machine with a huge diagonal boom extending into the willows. It had no treads, being merely ancillary, a hoister of bundled logs with no mobility of its own. Scratched across its yellow base was the name "Pete."

"Meet the Cosmic Copulator," Ben said. "Specializing in one-night stands. Not much left of his insides. He's been our prime source of copper. The last batch of speculators left him behind when they cleared out."

He waxed eloquent about a 1940 Chevy truck rusting on its rims, but paid little attention to the spider web that spanned the space between the wheel and the dirver's seat. A literary cliché, to be sure, but a lot more beautiful to me than the rusty old truck.

He was triumphant when he extricated not only a rusty oil drum but a length of rubber hose from the Chevy's engine, which would serve, he said, as a drain pipe. To show me just how he intended to build the bath, he squatted on the sand and drew a rough sketch with a stick. The drum would be mounted on a ring of stones enclosing a fire; the drain pipe would carry the soapy water off, so as not to put the fire out. "If you had a pith helmet and a pair of eyeglasses, you could pretend you were a missionary," I said.

"I'm going to build a wooden platform inside, and steps going up on the outside, so the hot rim won't catch you at the groin."

"Catch *you* at the groin," I corrected him.

He was very high on his discoveries. "I told you, *every-*

thing's here!" he cried, and, picking up a length of iron pipe from the ground, he struck the side of the propane tank once, twice, and then a third time. Like a gong, its vibrations echoed against the hills. "Gilly's front door bell," he whispered.

Miles away a dog barked.

"They're home," he said. "Let's go!"

The road on the other side of the campground was lined with young alders touching and mingling overhead, a domestic, well-drained road such as one would find in the backwoods of Vermont. I trailed a good twenty paces behind Ben, stopping to look at lavender blossoms on invisible stems, at yellow violets in the grass. "Things come back," these gentle flowers said to me. "Even out of ruins." There were deer tracks on damp places on the road, and wolf tracks as well. Wherever there was one, there was the other.

About a mile between the Ruins and the shore of Forsook Lake, Ben said we could cut a considerable distance by crossing a logjam, if I were willing.

The logjam looked like the elephant's graveyard in a Tarzan movie. Bone-white snags clawed up one another's backs. Trees as thick as mastodons wallowed in the water. Grasping at branches, roots, burls, at anything sticking more than two feet out of the water, I crawled across on all fours, reverting, like the terrain, to a lower and wilder order.

On the other bank, a short distance away, a low, flat span divided Lesser Forsook Lake from Greater Forsook Lake. It was a spillway, the same sort of structure which once raised the level of Tibbett Lake and drowned the trees along the shore. Made of three sections of timber, each of them four feet wide, it was bolted together by yard-long spikes. Paul Bunyan and his Blue Ox Babe could have departed only a little while ago. I pictured brawling lumberjacks just down the road, eating pancakes and cursing the task that made them heroes. But there were no donkey engines steaming and chucking, no hoarse cries, no creaking ropes. A ghostly silence lay over the bridge, and berry bushes sprouted from its seams.

The meadow that lay between the end of the dam and Gilly's woods smelled of hot grass and damp earth. Entering her forest on the land side instead of from the lake, it was as if the doors to a cathedral swung slowly open. Ancient cedars, widely spaced and airy, held up the roof, half of whose supporting pillars had crashed, ages ago, to the earth. Great patches of sunlight poured through the holes in the ceiling, carving baroque adornments on the massive vertical forms. A little plastic house, transparent and colorful as a soap bubble, stood on the brown forest floor and before it, ax in hand, stood Gilly, her red hair aflame like an icon.

"Christ!" she cried, running toward me with outstretched arms, "What took you so goddamned long?"

While we hugged one another, I spotted a loaf of dark brown bread standing on the table of her house. Disengaging myself, I darted inside and crammed a thick piece into my mouth and felt a stab of envy, surveying the gallon-jars of white rice and brown, of beans, dried peas, macaroni, raisins, nuts, apricots, peanut brittle, cheese chunks, figs, flour, sugar, oil, soybeans, and cornmeal ranged in rows beneath the kitchen counter. Either Gilly's mother was placating her conscience with substantial checks, or Gilly's new husband came from a rich, indulgent family. Unlike Ben's place, Gilly's was hung with bright, handwoven fabrics—Mexican, Indian, and Greek—glowing with color and pattern. Large baskets overflowed with shoes and caps and woolen mittens, new rainjackets hung from the beams. There was a sleeping loft, a shelf the size of a double bed built across the width of the house, and blankets drooped loosely over the edge. It was a larger house than Ben's, hexagonal in shape, like a gazebo, and flooded with sunshine.

"How's Ellis?" Ben asked, taking a seat on the log that Gilly was chopping when we arrived. They spoke to one another slowly and cautiously. Gilly leaned against her doorpost and said "He's okay. Be back soon. He's off in the woods with Armstrong." And rolled herself a cigarette with red, tobacco-stained fingers.

On the ground outside the house, and on the trunks of fallen, moss-covered trees, little caches of used dishes and kitchen utensils were assembled, as if at the end of each meal things were carted outside until a decision could be reached about who was to wash them. Meanwhile a fat, shiny slug undulated over ridges of left-over macaroni and cheese in a shallow Melmac bowl.

Gilly had certainly reverted to type since my abortive attempt to reform her last year. Except for her delicate complexion and her smooth, lovely neck, she looked like a boy.

A year ago, when I thought I'd persuaded her to give up on Ben, she had asked my help in getting an interesting literary job. She'd found an ad in a local paper for a night copy editor on a newspaper, and I was elated by the chance of saving her from wasting her life on dead-end dreams.

I had a great time that afternoon. I set her up with the *Manual of Style*, and she learned all the copy editor's marks in a quarter of an hour. She'd come to me straight from Vermont, where she'd spent the winter in a chicken coop trying to prove to Ben and to herself that she could be just as independent as he. She smelled like a chicken coop. I sent her upstairs with an armload of clean clothes borrowed from my daughter's closet, and bottles of shampoo, bubblebath, cologne, dusting powder, and hair conditioner: my daughter's. When she came down again she looked, and smelled, like a pink wild rose. "You'll knock them dead in Personnel," I predicted. But she looked so ravishing that the personnel manager thought she wouldn't be safe as the only woman in the plant on the night shift. So she took her own clothes back and got herself a job as a dogcatcher. Six months later she was back in B.C., settled in on Forsook Lake six miles away from Ben.

Ben admired her sturdy wood floor, reproaching himself again for not having put one in his own house before my arrival. "Yeah," she said with a low giggle, "next time it rains the whole place'll float away like a boat."

It nearly had, the week before. Gilly awoke one morning and found herself completely surrounded by water, her pots and dishes bobbing around, floating off. She still hadn't found them all.

"I really oughta move it to higher ground," she said without conviction. For she had built this little house entirely by herself. Ellis had had a separate house nearby, but when it collapsed under a load of snow he'd moved in with Gilly. She asked us to come and look at a sturdy shed she was building outside.

Twenty yards behind her house, an old snag, about

five feet in diameter, leaned toward her house, precisely in its line of fall.

"Gilly, you've *got* to move the house immediately! Do you see that tree?" I seized her arm, visions of Harry Fox looming before my eyes.

"Aw, no," she said, bland as could be, "that tree's been leaning like that for at least two hundred years. I figure my karma'd have to be *pretty weak* for it to fall over while I'm inside."

Gilly did not share my urgency about food, for, as soon as she'd showed us the shed, she resumed her position holding up the doorpost. "Gilly, be a dear and make us a cup of coffee," I said, drawing on my past credit. She poked about among the dishes on the shelf, searching for a coffee pot, and made no comment when Ben drew the clam chowder concentrate and the venison from his backpack and took over the preparation of lunch.

"I been expecting you for a whole week" she said to me reproachfully.

What did she hope for, I wondered? That I would unravel Ben? "But how did you know I was here?"

"Heard the plane. Anybody else, they'd 've just dumped 'em off at the float, but they took *you* right up to the door."

Ellis came out of the woods accompanied by Armstrong, a large black and white dog who barked loudly at a distance. The dog was handsome, overdressed—like a doorman. Gilly's husband was a loose-limbed young man with a great mass of curly golden hair, a scant golden beard, a curly golden smile, and thin, gold-rimmed spectacles with flat lenses that gave his face the double-zero look of Little Orphan Annie. "Mmmmm, clam chowder!" he exclaimed, shoving aside an opened copy of *Women in Love* and sliding into the nearest chair and helping himself to a steaming bowl. "Yummy!" He interrupted himself long enough to offer me a limp handshake—to inquire "Have a nice trip?" —and pursued the nourishment with enthusiasm.

The talk grew easier with Ellis there. Did Ben know that MaryLou and Dunc had checked out of their place on Capaswap Lake because the noise of the road-building was getting on her nerves? That Diana wanted to move the shakes out before the meeting with Swen? "I saw Swen over at Capaswap last week," Ellis said. "He was plowin' up the creek with a bulldozer. What a fuckin' mess!"

"It's against their religion to do anything by hand," Gilly said to me wryly.

Ellis stretched his long, thin arms above his head, arched his back, and yawned extravagantly. " 'f we sell the shakes down in Vancouver, it'll teach the Company a good lesson," he said.

Their cracker-barrel caucus, with its long intervals of silence, it sage shakings of the head, its determined ignorance of the ways of the world, bored me to death. They gave me a bellyache. I did not inquire into the location of Gilly's facility but wandered outside to look at the forest. It was a spooky woods. Windfalls as high as my chest lay prone, the sarcophagi of giants, adorned with ferns and moss. Vertical root systems, still protesting ancient separation, grappled like black snakes with the vacant air.

I found the stream that flowed behind Gilly's house and followed it beyond the tube of toothpaste lying on a grassy sandbar; climbing past a little falls, knowing that if I stayed within sight of running water I would not get lost. Gilly exasperated me, organizing her whole existence

around Ben's resistance, building this way station in which
to keep her passion in abeyance. And how could an intelligent, sensitive, literate, loony girl like Gilly endure Ellis?

A dense growth of evergreens, tall enough to be
gloomy but not tall enough to be grand, closed behind my
path. The brook became a washout, a dry, stony gully
where wild torrents had rushed, and later, withdrawn.
Marking the trail with my handkerchief, I headed into the
bush. Some sensors must have been developing in me while
I wasn't looking because, when I reached the spot toward
which I was heading, I discovered that it was, indeed, the
local facility.

"Keep an eye on her, will you?" Gilly's mother had
asked me before she moved permanently to Paris. Gilly's
mother had danced with Martha Graham and still wore her
hair in bangs, as in the olden days. "My husband says, 'Just
fit her with an IUD, and turn her loose,' but I don't think
that's all there is to it, do you?" I had been outraged by
Gilly's mother, at the implication that her daughter was the
victim of Ben's exploitation, that I should take responsibility for her child. She spoke of Gilly as if she were a package
she was leaving behind for me to mail. And why? Because
I was so powerful? So stable? So obviously an earth mother
who had nothing better to do than round up lost children?

"Off my back, Mrs. McMichael!" I wanted to reply.
But of course I said nothing of the kind. And, of course, the
moment the opportunity presented itself, I'd done precisely what she'd asked me to do. Because Gilly was a child,
a waif, and she could have been my daughter-in-law.

Ben was preparing to leave when I returned, stuffing
a jar of flour, a bottle of vegetable oil, and a can of coffee
into his backpack. The transaction was as impersonal as a
check-out counter at the Grand Union.

"And Gilly, can you loan me some wool, so I can fix Ben's sweater?" I asked.

We walked over to the new shed together. Balls of yarn lay in a large plastic bowl, tightly lidded. "Take as much as you want," she said. Then, in a thick whisper: "Christ, it's a good thing you got here. He never has anything to eat. He won't take anything, either, unless he pays it back. Makes everybody around here feel so goddamned guilty! Why does he make himself so damned . . . inaccessible?"

I might have turned the question around and asked "Why do you?", but I shrugged. "Search me," I replied.

I would not allow myself to think about his larder, about what he would do when Gilly's cooking oil and flour and coffee ran out, and I had diced and fried the last onion. Even if his larder were not completely empty, what proof would a cup of dried milk powder or an inch or two of oil be against a summer coming, and a fall and a winter after that? How would he live after I was gone? How would I manage to smile when the moment came for me to kiss him good-bye?

"Stop!" I told myself. "Don't spoil it. Just think about now."

Ellis and Gilly offered to take us across Forsook Lake in their canoe, leaving a woebegone Armstrong howling on the shore. Ben picked up his steel drum and rubber hose at the Ruins, carrying the drum overhead like a porter on a safari. Ellis carried along his saw, and as we neared the float at Tibbett Lake he swiped at inch-thick saplings near the shore with the whining blade. "Waaaagh! Waaagh!"

He and Gilly stood on the float as Ben untied the canoe. Gilly scratched at her crotch and said "Jesus, I'm dying for a hot bath."

We were pulling away from the float when Ben looked

up and said, as if it were an afterthought, "Come over in a couple of days. It'll take me a couple of days to build the bath."

We paddled in silence down Tibbett Lake, our oars moving in perfect unison. When we were out of earshot Ben said, "Why don't you like Ellis, Mom?"

"Did it show? I didn't mean it to. . . ." Which made him laugh. "Maybe because he isn't nutty like you and Buddhi and Gilly. He's got no . . . shadows. He isn't driven by anything except what's in front of his nose."

"Ellis isn't a bad sort. He's just young. His parents were sore as hell when he married Gilly. You have to be tolerant of people up here. There are so few of us. We have to get along."

"Gilly's another story. Can you tell me, Ben, what it is between you and Gilly?"

He debated with himself for a while before speaking. "I don't know; everything I do, she does. I build a house so she builds a house, except that she puts hers on low ground right in the way of a snag. I build a kayak, so she builds a kayak, only she uses the wrong glue and all the struts get sprung. Then she wants me to fix it for her. One mess after another. It just gets to the point where it's either her or me. We get along great for a day or two and then . . . bang!"

The wrong glue. Who can argue when it comes to glue?

Her, or him? There was no other choice in the wilderness. In the wilderness you could not afford to be a romantic. There was no margin here for error. If Gilly was always going to put herself in the path of falling timber, if she was always going to place herself in iron cradles, hoping the doors of the monastery would open and take her in, would it help if Ben moved her house? Picked up her clothes? Washed her dishes? Mended her kayak? No more than it changed her when I sent her upstairs to take a bubble bath.

"But I'm glad, Ben, that you did ask her to come over to take a bath. I didn't think you were going to."

"Well . . ." he said, and I heard him sigh.

"It just goes to show," I thought to myself with some satisfaction, "like mother, like son."

Ben spent the next few days constructing a short flight of steps to lead up to the rim of the steel drum and a shelf to step down to, inside it. He cut a slice of cedar for a circular platform to protect his feet and weighed it down with a large rock. The most difficult problem was to fit the rubber hose into the base of the drum snugly enough so that the water would not leak out and douse the fire. The hose was open-ended, of course, and had to be fastened in an upright position so that gravity or capillary attraction or water seeking its own level—some such principle— would keep the bath full long enough for the bather to get wet all over. I never witnessed the scheme in operation, for, while Ben immersed himself in warm water, I retired to the Kiosk with a book and an oil lamp and listened to the bugs battering themselves against my transparent walls. But the claims Ben made for his bath were large.

It was time for the vegetables to sprout. I went down to the garden, searching for evidence of genuine Swiss chard, honest-to-goodness beets, a believable carrot, but there was no sign that Mother Nature had heard our prayers. I'd begun to pull a few of the flourishing weeds when I thought I heard a whistle, and a human voice, coming from beyond the fringe of cedar boughs that lined the shore. There was a flash of color through the foliage and the sound of a large object thrashing in the underbrush.

". . . call this a goddamn path? How're ya s'posed to get through here?"

The voice was Gilly's. She was stuck on the other side of a dense tangle of vines. "Yay! Gilly's here!" I shouted up to Ben, and flung myself into the brush to give her a hand, to pull her into the clearing.

"Gosh!" Ben cried, hurrying down the hill, "the social life around here's increasing by leaps and bounds!"

Gilly had walked all the way over from Capaswap Lake and around the rim of Tibbett Lake.

"But at least, Gilly, you'll get to have a hot bath!" I said.

"Hot diggety-dawg!" she exclaimed.

Ben made a fuss over Gilly, brought her a cup of tea on a saucer while she rested on the ground, hauled half a dozen buckets of water down from the spring to fill the oil drum, chopped a pile of wood for a fire. They smoked and laughed together, old buddies from away back when. Ellis was just the neighbor on Forsook Lake who'd taken Dale's boat over to the lighthouse, to see if he could contact a company to take the shakes down to Vancouver. Just a parenthetical remark in a continuing conversation.

We ate a big, jolly supper together, after which I made as many disappearances as possible, considering the limitations inherent in the situation. I weeded the garden until my back gave out, then climbed up to the Kiosk and brought one of my two foam rubber mattresses down for Gilly to sleep on. Without comment, I put it on the workbench next to Ben's.

"Take that back," he whispered to me when Gilly was out of earshot.

"But why? She can't sleep on bare wood!"

"She's *used* to sleeping on bare wood. You're not. You'll never sleep unless you have both of 'em on your bed."

"Oh, for Christ's sake, Ben!" I said, and gave him a dirty look. I did not take it back. I retired, instead, to the Kiosk, bearing an oil lamp aloft and thinking how spartan for sex to be surrounded by saws and chisels and mallets.

When we met in the clearing next morning, Gilly said she'd had a marvelous bath the evening before, that she felt simply great. I noted that Ben had slept on a pile of balsam boughs inside the house and had given Gilly his own bed on the workbench. Nobody had used the second mattress.

Gilly would have stayed on, I was perfectly sure, if only Ben had asked her. She began the construction of a tall stool, just like those Ben had made for his own house, but watching her work I could see that she had no knack with tools. She must have built that house of hers out of sheer doggedness. Clearly, Ben admired her spunk, her intelligence, but there was something missing between them. The right glue? It wasn't that she lacked the helplessness of traditional femininity. Quite the contrary. What seemed to put Ben off as they worked side by side was the fact that she called on him continuously for help. She was too needy. She required too much of his attention. By the middle of the afternoon, I could see that his patience was wearing thin.

"I'll take you across in the canoe," he volunteered, "so you can get home before dark."

"See you in a couple of days," she said to me, for Ellis

was sure to have found a shipper and we would soon be going to Capaswap to move the shakes down to Camp Nought.

Wrapping her arms around me, she left a little patch of wet on the back of my neck.

"What can you do, Gilly?" I said, for there was something heart-piercing in the way she brushed away a tear that slid underneath her glasses. "I just wish . . ."

She put her arm around my shoulder as we walked downhill together toward the canoe.

"Good ol' Mom," she said in a husky voice as I kissed her good-bye.

11

How often in the past Ben had reproached me for my obsession with time, with time's utility! To him, my life appeared to be a chopped-up, anxiety-ridden race against time. The moment I broke through one tape with my chest, I immediately organized another competition.

It was not as if I didn't understand that it was equally futile to try to stretch time, or to pack it with events. The more you stretched it, the thinner it became. And the more you packed it with events, the more all the events began to resemble one another. I'd tried, through reading Chinese philosophy and a little bit of Zen, to put myself into another dimension, to feel a timeless sort of time. In vain.

Yet I must have been slipping into a new rhythm because I did not know where the time was going. Apart from inserting the two squares into Ben's sweater, I did nothing I could remember doing.

The rhythm of Ben's life altered, too. "It's a big adjustment, getting up so early in the morning," he observed. "I could save a lot on lamp oil if I didn't stay awake half the night. The one trouble with this place is that it's dark. Mountains on both sides. The next house I build is going to get the morning sun."

I'd have been content with idleness, but after a while Ben said we ought to set up temporary housekeeping at the Civic Center at Capaswap in order to be on hand whenever it was generally decided to move the shakes down to Camp Nought.

A gentle rain was falling the morning we packed the canoe for our departure. Heavy mist lay over the mountains, and the canoe shone dully against the gray green waters of Tibbett Lake. It was a hushed, insulated morning. All the outlines were blurred.

We cut diagonally across the lake, headed southwest into a still lagoon enclosed by steep hills. Hundreds of deadheads of varying height stood in the water, and a couple of ducks took wing as we approached. The canoe slid, sibilant, between clumps of tall, orange reeds, brushed over lily pads on intricate stems. It was like floating over the surface of a Chinese porcelain, looking through the glaze into the original design, entering the elusive element, *is-ness*.

The taut strings eased. Energy poured through my being. The last dot was placed on the perimeter of a circle. In the profound peace of this perfection, I thought, "It would be all right to die now, if this is how it feels to give up struggling with time. . . ."

Ben tied the canoe to a stout root that looped out from

the shore and hid the paddles in the underbrush. The path began with a calisthenic climb over loose earth and torn roots, up the side of a peninsula which rose almost vertically from the lagoon. Dripping water pattered the sounds of the forest, falling branch-to-branch from trees lost at the top in cloud. We came out of the woods onto an old road facing a broken tree whose severed trunk pointed straight toward us, like the muzzle of a big, black cannon.

Half a mile from the canoe, we began to hear the noise of the Company's road builders, but they were still far from sight. Ben said it took two hours longer to get to Capaswap in summertime because this road was so densely overgrown with salmonberry, thimbleberry, blackberry, and other edible growth, and he was never able to escape the temptation to stuff himself along the way.

A small gorge bisected the road where a boil of water altered its direction and cut into the earth, exposing a great jumble of root and rock. A single, square beam lay across the gorge, but on the farther side was the beginning of a broad, planked platform. Ben helped me inch my way across, cautioning me not to look at my feet. "We never finished this bridge," he said. "This is where we came to a parting of the ways with the government."

While I sat on a boulder, insulated from the wet by rain pants, Ben drew his father's penknife from a pocket and cut a few slips from a willow growing beside the noisy stream. Buds were just beginning to appear on the slips, and Ben stuck them into the raw, exposed earth of the bank. "Maybe they'll root, hold the soil."

Some time ago, he'd written me that his group had received a government grant to survey the creeks on Proctor's Island, measure the water levels, count the fish, estimate the tonnage of timber presently blocking the passage of fish to the spawning grounds.

"They really did hassle us," he told me now. "What's the sense in just writing a report, if you don't do anything about the conditions? See, this is still a pretty passable road, except at this point. We had to get some machinery through to start pulling windfalls off the creek. We tried doing it by hand, but me and Ellis spent a whole day and we didn't even move one log. So we began by rebuilding this bridge. The timber was all here, but it had washed out. We were halfway through when some bureaucrats from Manpower came to see what we were doing with their money. Decided we were misappropriating the funds, that we must have some other, sinister, purpose in mind, so they started investigating everybody. The RCMP . . . the works. We called a meeting. The Co-op voted, unanimously, to give all the money back."

"To do *what?*"

"Give it back!"

"Don't you realize, Ben, that in the entire history of organized society, *nobody* has ever given back a government grant? Why, it probably cost five times whatever they laid out to invent a new accounting procedure! And what happened to the survey?"

"It's down in some office in Vancouver."

He stared into the gully, then stretched a crumpled plastic covering over a quantity of loose nails rusting on the unfinished surface of the bridge. "We should have fought it out," he said thoughtfully. "But no one was willing to waste the time sitting in stuffy government offices, trying to find the right guy to talk to. Maybe I should have done it. But they'd have said, 'That punk, that American.' So I didn't do it, either."

About a mile and a half from Tibbett Lake, the old road merged with a newer one. We crossed an ugly, efficient bridge with a huge, concrete culvert beneath it, and a ravaged beaver dam. The beavers hadn't left even after the place was plowed to bits. They were starting a new dam, right up against the culvert, on the upstream side. I'd have been happy to sit on the bridge for a few hours to see if a real live beaver would show up and smack his tail on the water, but Ben was in a hurry to get to Capaswap Lake. We would sleep at the Civic Center, and he needed some time to make it habitable.

A vast mud pile marked the place where Swen Mohring was clearing out a creek bed with a bulldozer. As Ellis had said, it was an indescribably bloody mess. Chunks and globs of mud, piles of roots altered the terrain beyond all hope of defining the water course.

It was too misty to see Capaswap Lake, but we could hear it chuck-chucking beyond a border of trees. Ben showed me a crumple of plastic sheeting on the right side of the road. It belonged to a Japanese-Canadian photographer by the name of Scott Woriaki. "A most ingenious structure, made entirely of string and plastic. Like a cat's cradle. You just pull one string and the whole house balloons out. I don't know if he's planning to come back here or not this summer."

"Why not?"

"The string broke," he replied.

By comparison with where Ben lived, the shore of Capaswap Lake was a thriving metropolis. Scott's was one of four houses on the southern shore. A five-minute paddle across the lake, or a twenty-minute walk around it, lay Dale's digs, described by Ben as being the oldest and most luxurious accommodations on the island. Farther, the road on which we dodged puddles continued for another five miles and connected Capaswap Lake with Camp Nought, another abandoned logging camp which now served the Co-op as a seaport. Moreover, there was even an existing vehicle for traversing that road. She was called "Ruby" or the "Power Wagon"—a flatbed truck with a smashed windshield, torn fenders, a cockeyed bumper, and a load of bundled cedar shakes strapped to her back. When Ben greeted her with a pat on the hood, I expected her to beep in reply; she had that much personality.

Ruby stood in the driveway of a building about the same size and shape as Gilly's, except that it had a well-shingled roof. Save for the cold, rusty Airtight in the middle of the floor and one large, slope-backed armchair, it was empty of furnishings. There was a sleeping loft supported by two thick posts, and underneath shelves crowded with books and a variety of odd containers. The kitchen was a rough plank mounted on blocks, with a propane stove and a few utensils. It was dingy with disuse like the kitchen of an unheated church basement.

As I stood outside the Center looking in, a helmeted man in dark glasses roared past on a motorcycle. He did not turn his head by a hair to acknowledge my presence.

"Is it against Company rules to look at the locals?" I asked Ben.

"They're all like that, pretty much," he said with a shrug, and ordered me up into the loft to take a nap.

Not the hauling of water, the sweeping of floor, the splitting of firewood, the baking of fresh bread in the Airtight, nor the starting up and dying away of a gasoline engine in the driveway aroused me. I was dreaming an important dream:

Seven bushels of Northern Spy apples stood on the floor of my kitchen back home. The *I Ching* lay open on the counter, like a recipe book; but the counter was not formica, it was the split cedar log in Ben's little house. Ben held yarrow stalks in his hand. "I don't know if I can get an accurate answer on this surface," he was saying. "It's alive!" I understood he meant there was an emanation of energy from the wood, which might alter the way the stalks moved in midair.

"Never mind," I urged him, "Just ask if I should make applesauce."

He tossed the stalks into the air and studied the position of their fall. "It comes out Number One in the Sign of the Creative!" he exclaimed.

"Never mind what the sign is," I said, annoyed. "What does it say about applesauce?"

Before he replied in my dream, a sharp little voice directly beneath me piped, "You wanna see my silver cup, Ben?"

I guessed it must be Astri Finn. She was clad in a tiny, yellow slicker. Her red rubber boots were on the wrong feet, her rainhat was inside out, plopped crookedly on her head. Tiny blue jeans were fastened at the waist with a safety pin, which appeared to be endangering her belly button, and she was holding up, for Ben's inspection, a tin-foil cup smaller than her thumb.

"I made it out of a cigarette package from the road," she said, standing on tiptoe to keep a proprietory eye on her creation. Ben tried to stand it on the shelf, next to a water glass with a bunch of fresh, pink flowers in it. "I'm giving it to Diana," she said, reaching to reclaim her creation. Ben praised it without condescension, and she returned outdoors with a jaunty, self-sufficient walk. Where did she get the idea of fashioning a silver goblet? Who had ever spoken to this child of nature of candlelit dinners? Religious ceremonies? Magic chalices? Had the idea come to her from books? A genetic code? A collective feminine unconscious?

I pulled myself together in a hurry. A man I took to be Astri's father, Dale, was lying under the Power Wagon with the soles of his black boots sticking out. Her brother Jimmy was riding around and around in the driveway on a new bicycle with colored plastic ribbons at the ends of the handlebars, yelling "Gggggggggrrrrrrrr! Awrrrrr!" Ben was talking about Ruby's brake linings when I came out. "Hey, Astri," Ben said, "This is my mother."

"Your *mother?*" she screamed, grabbing herself around the middle and doubling over with laughter. "How could you have a *mother?*"

"She's the second person here who thinks it's funny, so maybe it is . . ." I said to Ben.

Jimmy stopped riding the bike long enough to extend his little hand according to remembered instructions, but Astri regarded me soberly and kept her distance. She had a round face, skin as brown as a walnut shell, very rosy cheeks, and incredibly bright eyes. "That was a beautiful cup you made, Astri," I said. But she was not to be taken in by empty flattery. "I know it," she said, and turned away.

Dale wriggled out from under the truck. He was short and slight, clean-shaven with a graven, dark-complected face. He acknowledged Ben's introduction with a shy, guarded smile, summoned his children to get ready to leave, and spoke further to Ben about moving the shakes out tomorrow. He and Diana had put the first load on

Ruby's back a few days earlier, to get a head start on the operation.

"See you tomorrow," he said with a half-salute. He and Astri had exactly the same walk, short-legged and nimble, tightly packed with energy. They disappeared into the bushes, descending by a path through the woods to the lake shore. I could hear both children chattering at once, then Astri's high, clear voice asking her father, "Can I bring Potlatch tomorrow, to show her?"

" 'Potlatch' is her black cat," Ben explained.

"What a child!"

"Yeah, Astri's something else. Her mother was the best shot on the island."

"Was? Isn't Diana her mother?"

"No, Dale and her mother broke up when she was born. Astri only lived with her for two years. Then her mother got fed up and sent her up to Dale. Pinned a card to her sweater saying 'Deliver to D. Finn,' and put her on a plane. Dale's had her ever since."

"And Diana?"

"Diana's great. A very together person. Not at all over-protective."

Ben slept on the ground floor of the Center, and I slept in the loft. Most of the heat from the Airtight collected under the shingled roof, which was lined with reflective aluminum foil. It was a drowsy-making roost, with an oil lamp and pillows to prop against the back, good for a long read.

There were plenty of good books on the shelves, contemporary fiction and classics, and an interesting collection of nonfiction, including one book I'd written myself. I was inordinately pleased to find it and warbled on and on about my far-flung readership.

"Even Ray Beame's read a couple of your books. He's the keeper of the lighthouse at Fairharbor.

"You loaned them to him, you mean."

"No, the government sent them. They send crates of books at a time to people in the bush."

"You mean he read them voluntarily, and not because he knew you and I were related?"

"He didn't know it when he read them. It took about six months before he actually got around to asking Dale, straight out, if I was your son. People don't talk about things like that so easily around here."

"Why is everybody so secretive? Are they all fleeing some dark, secret past?"

"No, it's that so few big things happen here. When something does, you have to stretch it out as long as you can. It would be very wasteful to use something like that up, all in one conversation."

It was still raining the next morning. Ben cooked a mess of hominy grits and a sulfurous concoction of powdered eggs for breakfast, making extravagant claims for the taste, largely unsupported by the evidence. The meal lay in my stomach like an anchor, and I was glad I had nothing more to do than to lie in bed the rest of the day and read.

By midmorning Gilly and Ellis straggled down the road, one at a time, with sleeping bags and backpacks strapped to themselves. They were going to spend the night next door, in the house left vacant by the couple who could not tolerate the noise.

Astri came into the Center to show me her cat, Potlatch. I took a big risk in telling her I was afraid of cats, not only of black cats but of all cats. Would she mind very much leaving Potlatch outside? Without surprise or ceremony, she dumped Potlatch on the outside of the door flap. The next time I looked at her, she was standing under the sleeping loft combing her hair with an old, broken-toothed comb, smug as a movie queen.

Diana came in next and introduced herself. She was a serious-looking girl with horn-rimmed glasses, long, blonde hair, slender build, and a straightforward manner. She accepted a cup of hot tea from me and slumped into the big chair, regarding me with round, dark eyes.

"Ben's an amazing person," she said. "A really amazing person. The best there is. But why does he live that way? As if he were expiating some kind of a sin?"

"I wish . . . I knew," I murmured. Gilly clomped in, said to Diana, "What's the matter? You're lookin' so down!"

"Feelin' down," Diana replied, and seemed on the verge of tears. "Today's my birthday. I feel so *old!*" She drew out the last word, *Oooooollllld!*

"Congratulations," I said. "How old are you?"

"Twenty-twwwwooooo!"

When I patted her smooth hair and smiled, she looked up and said wistfully, "Do you know, you're the first mother who's ever come up here? Say, do you think you could fix a mistake I made in a sweater? Gilly says you're a good knitter."

"I'd love to, Diana. It would make me feel useful."

"Oh, you're plenty useful," she said, exchanging a knowing glance with Gilly. "Don't have to worry about that!"

Ellis and Dale and Ben came into the Center and stood around the Airtight smoking and sipping hot tea. After a while the talk took the form of a roundtable, with Dale sitting on a straight-backed chair like a chairman, the Tide Book open in his lap. I climbed back into the loft to listen. The longer they talked, the clearer it became that they were not only underequipped with manpower, they were uncertain about transporting the shakes from Camp Nought to a point of sale, they had no idea what the shakes were worth, they had no customer for the product. Even I knew that in business you sewed up the sale first, and worried about the product later. That you put the risk on the buyer, and not on the seller. Didn't Dale know that? Wasn't he a man of the world? But as far as I could see, all the wisdom and leadership Dale had to contribute was the chart in the Tide Book which told precisely the time at which an old float at Camp Nought would be lying horizontally on the waters of Dyer Strait, and at what hour it would be hanging on the pile of rock to which it was anchored. Like the Spirit of Sisyphus.

"What's to stop someone from ripping off the shakes?" Gilly asked. "Anybody passing by in a boat could . . ."

"Ray could keep an eye on them from the lighthouse," someone said.

"How far away is that lighthouse from Camp Nought?" I inquired from upstairs.

"Only eight miles, the other side of the strait," someone replied.

Then there was the question of where the shakes could be stored, presuming that the coastal steamer did pick them up as promised.

Ben suggested storing them on a ramp in a park thirty

miles north of Vancouver. He knew a guy there who was building a boat.

"In a public park?"

"Yeah, George. He lives in a tree, eighty feet above ground. No one's ever climbed up to get him out. He'd be glad to keep an eye on the shakes. . . ."

"I think you may need a permit to leave 'em in a public park," Ellis said.

"There's another thing," Dale said. He spoke softly, with some reluctance. "Swen hasn't tagged the last batch of shakes yet. Three quarters of the shakes have tags, but not the last ones. We could try to sell them without, but the hassles . . ."

Buddhi appeared like a ghost in the driveway. He entered the Center silently, rain dripping from his cape. His rubber sandals slapped noisily against the wooden floor. He looked detached again, as if he'd delivered only his body to the work site; nodded to every one, and turned to the book shelf where he thumbed through one volume after another in complete and self-absorbed silence. His arrival seemed to flip a switch in Diana.

"Listen," she said in a low, strained voice. "We can sit around here for the next ten days scaring the shit out of one another. We've been talking about this for two years. For Christ's sake, let's *do* something for a change!"

Her words hung in the room like a layer of smoke. No one replied, acknowledged her outburst, argued. Someone passed a reefer and everybody took a drag, dampening their aggression while they dealt with the question of whether or not to commit themselves to taking another step. No one, with the exception of Diana, would risk persuasion, criticism, accusation, no one would press anyone else to the limits of their commitment. Stretching, yawning, they moved about the space like sleepwalkers, as if to demonstrate that Diana's impatience could not, possibly, have any effect upon their behavior. In this way, Diana need feel no guilt, either. They were all catatonic with self-determination.

"Suppose you took a photograph of all of you, standing in front of the shakes. Wouldn't that constitute legal evidence?" I inquired from the loft.

"I think my camera's still here, somewhere," Ben said, and slipped out into the rain.

"Me and Gilly could sleep on the float tonight," Ellis said, "until the guy comes with the boat . . ."

Indeed, Ben did come up with one of my husband's old cameras in hand. All the young people left the Center and stood around in the driveway. "Get closer together, so I can get everybody in," Ben said, peering into the camera.

"Me too!" cried Astri, whose father picked her up and placed her on Ruby's hood. Everybody shuffled closer together, everybody looked in Ben's direction, and everybody smiled. He snapped the shutter.

At once, the group dispersed, galvanized into motion. Ellis seized a long steel pike and climbed on top of the shakes; Gilly followed him, rain streaming down her yellow slicker, down her pink, smiling cheeks. Rain glistened on Ellis's eyeglasses, coursed through his golden beard. Armstrong ran back and forth in the driveway, barking and winding his plumed, white tail. Potlatch scooted into the Center and scooted out again just as fast. Buddhi stood a little aside, watching Dale and Diana pile the children, with their clattering metal lunch pails, into the front seat of the Power Wagon, and climb in after, one on either side.

Ben's cheeks were shiny, red apples. He did a jig of general joy in the driveway, then ran back into the house to leave the camera and say good-bye to me. Dale started the motor. Ruby shook violently. Her wheels were sunk six inches into mud. The engine died before Ben joined Ellis and Gilly and Buddhi on top of the shakes.

"Try it in second!" Ellis yelled.

Dale turned the motor over again. Except for Armstrong, protesting his imminent separation from Ellis, there was dead silence in the driveway.

Then Dale must have done something tricky with the clutch, for there was a great roar, the muffler emitted a cloud of dense, blue smoke, Ruby trembled, faltered, then lurched out of her rut, sending the loose figures on top sprawling into one another's arms. "Hang on, everybody!" Ben cried as the Power Wagon rocked out of the driveway, accompanied by loud cheers from all the passengers.

And one small hurrah, from the dry side of the plastic. The back of the camera had fallen open on the kitchen shelf. As I might have guessed, there wasn't any film inside.

12

I had to hand it to him. It was pure inspiration for him to have pretended there was film in the camera, to draw everyone together with an illusion. They were so gay, so enchanted, riding high on hope, barreling out of the driveway. Perhaps it didn't matter whether or not they would make any money on the sale of the shakes. Maybe the shakes were only the outward manifestation, and the thing that really counted was the spirit.

Yes, Ben was still tying unlikely things together with invisible strings. The whole idea of the Coastal Environment Cooperative was simply another of his concraptions, a wooden giraffe which he could manipulate by pulling strings. Making a living was no more serious to him than plucking dollar bills from the fingers of indulgent neighbors. It was half game, half cause. An existential excercise whose long-range object was to benefit the forest and whose short-range purpose was to see if he could get it to work. Starting every process from scratch, taking nothing on outer authority, he behaved as if he had a century in which to grow to maturity.

It was still early in the day. There was wood in the box and a fire in the Airtight. Last night, for the very first time, I'd succeeded in lighting both the propane stove and the Airtight, and I felt competent about staying behind alone, especially with Armstrong hanging around outside to guard me. Not that he and I had anything to say to one another. He was a one-man dog, an Alaskan Malemute; the only one who counted in his life was Ellis. Nevertheless, he was there.

Potlatch, on the other hand, took an immediate fancy to me. What is it with cats? A cat will run a mile from someone who yearns to hold it and pet it, but, let someone who doesn't care for cats turn up, and cats are drawn to that person as if by a magnet. Potlatch displayed just such an insane attachment to me. I threw her out of the loft five times, six, but she crept back up a seventh. Finally we attained an uneasy truce: she settled on the foot of my sleeping bag while I retired behind the history of a settlement on the northern tip of Vancouver Island, circa 1910. The history was dry enough to allow me to keep one eye on Potlatch and absorbing enough to make me forget that I was the only human being in approximately a hundred square miles.

It was edifying to read about Cape Scott. Unlike the shake splitters on the Power Wagon, its settlers knew what they were doing. They were experienced, practical people of high moral purpose, wholehearted in their commitment. They worked at the building of their colony not only one month out of every year, but twelve, and six days of the week out of seven, resting only to keep the Sabbath holy. An entire congregation, one hundred families from Ohio or Indiana, left their fat, fertile farm lands to hack a new life out of the tough, tangled, salal-infested soil of northern Vancouver Island. They built cabins, boats, a wharf; shot game, fished the warm waters of the Japan Current that swirled around Vancouver Island and produced the fog. And why? Because they wanted to live a pure life, to escape the sins of their neighbors.

They survived in spite of the broken promises of an ineffective government, which never came through with the roads, the schools, the medical services, the steamer connection the settlers counted on. They put up with isolation, exhaustion, hunger, heartache, cold, and death, because they were true believers, because they were a group, because they were capable of committing themselves to an idea that each of them felt was greater than they were.

Among the colonists was a woman who loved to play the piano. When the colony was still young, the first houses barely built, she sent for her piano, all the way back home to Ohio. It arrived in Vancouver by rail, was transferred to a lumber boat for the journey north. The whole population of Cape Scott was on the wharf to witness the debarkation of the piano. The deck hands put it in a log-sling and swung it over the side of the boat. But the sling broke and the piano fell into the water. Did they leave it there to rust, for fishes to pluck lullabies from? They did not. They hauled it out of the water and carried it over four miles of dirt road, and after many months it dried out. For the next twenty years, all religious observances at Cape Scott were accompanied by a little musical offering. When the settlement finally floundered, the woman who played the piano was among the very last to leave.

I enjoyed reading about Cape Scott. It was a straightforward piece of history, and it laid the blame for a lot of unnecessary suffering on the careless men who ran the government like a private gambling concession. There was something very wholesome and clear about the story. The victims were the good guys, their enemies were outsiders, men of power who failed to do their public duty. If any of the settlers had doubts, those doubts did not show up in the history.

Lighting out for the wilderness to escape the sins of one's neighbors, or one's fellow citizens, is a hallowed American impulse. Ever since the Pilgrim Fathers hit the Massachusetts shore, people have gotten fired up over the idea of a second chance. In those days, the East was the West. To Buddhists like Buddhi, the West had already become the East.

How naive, I thought as I closed the book, to think you can escape sin by a change in geography!

I ought to know because I'd tried it myself.

We had gone West by going north, to Montreal.

I, too, was full of piety, cloaking my terror and my despair with higher purposes.

"Remember, every one of you," I'd said to my children as we climbed out of the station wagon at the U.S.-Canada border to present our documents to the Canadian customs officer, "we are guests of this country. You will find many differences between Canada and the United States. You will observe, but you will not criticize, because you cannot possibly understand enough about Canada to pass any judgment. Respect your hosts and be grateful. Remember always that to Canadians you represent the United States. See to it that your behavior is worthy of the best traditions of our great country."

The customs officer reviewed our papers with pleasure. Most immigrants did not arrive at the border with comparable resources. He wished us a long and lucrative stay in Canada. "Lucrative, for *Canada,*" he specified with a laugh, and handed each of the younger children a lollipop. Ben was fourteen then. He was too old for a lollipop.

We moved into a house in the French part of Montreal, for I was avid for total ethnic immersion, for the exotic experience of "living abroad," thirty-five miles from Plattsburgh, New York. And made a number of quite painful discoveries, both about Quebec, and about ourselves.

"You Americans, you all have such good teeth!" a woman said to me at a dinner party. The statistic quoted everywhere was that, while the United States accounted for only six percent of the world's population, it consumed fifty-five percent of the world's product and energy. Of course, all Canadians deplored the Vietnam war and thought it praiseworthy that we, too, opposed the war. What baffled them was that we took it so much to heart. "When anything goes wrong here," they explained, "we refer it to a Royal Commission of Inquiry."

All the children talked about was the cruelty of teachers who practiced corporal punishment, and the stupidity of a school system whose administration was strictly parochial. There are no public schools in Quebec, in the sense Americans know them. All their conversations ended with a sigh, mourning the loss of a golden past, deploring their wintry present. One day I offered an extra dessert to anyone who brought a pleasant thought to the dinner table; I had no takers. "If you can't say anything nice, please don't say anything at all," I said, finally.

"Can't you bear a little adversity?" my husband would ask rhetorically. His homecoming each evening was the one bright spot in the day. While we waited for him we would sit in the drafty living room, the children and I, and watch the evening news. Watch the bombs plowing up the rice paddies, the expressionless men whipping out pistols and putting bullets through the heads of handcuffed prisoners. Night after night we watched women, carrying babies, fleeing across the gray screen with flames pouring from their backs.

When my husband came in, blue-faced and spent, we would all sit down to dinner together, warming our faces over the steam rising from our plates. Snow hissed against the black, uncurtained kitchen window. And the only other sound in the room was the sound of our strong, healthy American teeth, grinding, tearing our flavorfully cooked meat. It was the first time I realized that we were carnivores.

And Ben?

After dinner Ben would go up to his room on the second floor and close his door. Sometimes he played records. Usually there was no sound at all. Often, around midnight, he'd bundle up and go out walking in the snow. I didn't believe him when he said he went to an all-night Greek bakery, except that most of the time he'd come back at three or four in the morning carrying a bag of bagels.

He had a frightful time at school. He was sent to detention for not wearing a tie, for failing to call a teacher "Sir," for keeping a sloppy notebook. Detention was not the same as a study hall. No books were permitted in the room. No paper and no pencils. No company. It was pure vengeance.

"Can't you tell them, Mom?" he'd say to me. "Can't you ask them?"

"It's not our country," I'd reply. "It's not my place to criticize. We are guests here."

The day before Expo was to open—April, 1967—Ben came home from school looking happy and excited, for once. There was going to be an antiwar demonstration in front of the American consulate. We would all go, wouldn't we?

"Not unless I know who is sponsoring it," I said. He looked at me with astonishment.

I phoned several of the people who deplored the war at dinner parties, English-Canadian academics for the most part. "It's not the Canadian way to march in demonstrations," they all said. If I'd known any French academics to phone, they would have told me that the issue was not whether to march or not to march, but whether the signs denouncing the war would be written in English or in French.

If middle-class American liberals like us were not going to take part in the demonstration, who would be there? Draft resisters. Deserters. Radicals. And for every one of them, at least two men from the CIA.

"No, I think we will not go, Ben," I said, articulating each syllable with clarity and precision. "You see, dear, you have to look at it from the Canadian point of view. Expo is Canada's one hundreth birthday party. It's a great celebration of Canada's nationhood. Now, how would you feel about it if you were having a big birthday party and a bunch of outsiders came in and made a fuss over something that had nothing to do with you? You'd resent it, wouldn't you?"

Ben didn't argue, but he telephoned the boy who'd told him about the demonstration and asked if he would go with him. "No," the boy said after consulting with his mother, "I got a test tomorrow. I got to study." So nothing further was said.

After dinner I sat at the kitchen table and wrote a letter to my congressman saying, in essence, "I'm right behind you, Honorable Representative." Because he'd already taken a clear, brave stand against the war. Ben went up to his room and, I suspect, smoked a little grass. For less than half a dollar, each of us had purchased some peace of mind, but as far as the killing on the other side of the world was concerned, one action was indistinguishable from the other.

The next day, Ben showed me a one-inch story on the last page of the *Montreal Star* to the effect that twenty young men had attacked the American consulate with cardboard signs. They'd been dispersed by police on horseback. Three had been treated for concussion, but, since no damage to property had been reported, no arrests had been made.

As I recall, I played the piano a lot in those days.

It was very cold and damp in the Civic Center. The fire in the Airtight had gone out. I thought I'd fix myself a cup of hot tea. So I chased Potlatch off my feet and zipped myself out of the sleeping bag.

". . . as if he were expiating some kind of a sin," Diana had said.

There were only five matches in the matchbook. There was plenty of quartered wood, but no kindling. I went outside and looked around the driveway for small sticks, but there were very few and those I found were soaking wet. So I tried Ben's trick of making kindling by splintering an inch-square stick lengthwise with an ax. Except that, instead of holding it upright with a forefinger, I used a tin spoon. All I did was frighten Potlatch by flipping the spoon onto the floor, to produce one thin, raggedy splint. It was just too bleak, just too cold, just too much to cope with. One after the other, I lit all the matches and watched them all go out. When the last one curled up, I climbed back up into the loft. "What sin?" I asked myself. "Whose sin?"

Maybe I'd been looking in the wrong place, searching the scene of Ben's departure from home for clues. He must have reached bottom long before that, must have felt there was nothing to hang on to, nothing to believe in, least of all a mother who said to him: "No matter what your country does, it is your country. You are responsible to it. For it. None of us is better than our country." But if that country which you had already left, yet still must love, had become a nation of killers? If your own good teeth testified that you were a cannibal? That your wealth had been robbed from the poor of the world, to whom you were then offering cardboard boxes full of pennies? How many sixteen-year-olds were there who could work their way out of such a set of moral contradictions?

I knew very well the sin I had committed.

As the war wore on, there began to be not twenty American boys in Montreal, but hundreds. They slept in doorways, begged for nickels and dimes on Ste. Catherine Street. They had no money. They had no papers. They could not contact their families. They were not eligible for any kind of assistance. They had nowhere to live. The Canadian government did them the favor of pretending they were not there. The lucky ones got jobs at half the legal pay scale.

Any one of those boys could have been my son.

I could have helped them in a number of ways. I could have written letters to their families, offered housing, raised money. But I did not. I was afraid that the faceless apparatus which kept an eye on Americans abroad would finger me, that I would be accused of giving aid and comfort to "the enemy." That, out of revenge, my government would reach across the border and snatch away my sons. Oh, I had lots of other reasons for not doing anything, of course, but that was the only true reason.

I got a job at a Canadian university teaching contemporary literature. I was a sort of para-professional and earned so little that even the pettiest person in the English department could afford to overlook me. But anti-American feeling was strong in academe, and articulate. "Why don't the Americans take their fucking *Moby Dick* and get the hell out of here?" someone said at a faculty meeting, to hearty applause.

I even understood how they felt. If I had been a Canadian I might have felt the same way. Overshadowed by the American Presence.

But even that outpost of certified public accountancy had its moment of revolution. There were very few blacks in Canada. Less than one percent of the population and most of them from the British West Indies. A dozen West Indian students, suffering their own kind of isolation and anomie, finally demanded that the university treat them with the same consideration accorded white students, which was not asking a great deal by any standards. No liberal cracks appeared in the administration's armor. They rejected all the students' demands out of hand. In the resulting confrontation, the university's computer center was fried to a crisp. Of all the student revolts of the late

'60s, the destruction of the computer center was the most expensive, and the least illuminating, in North America. Nothing whatsoever was understood. Nothing whatsoever changed.

The fire department's ladders were still leaning up against the university building on the afternoon my husband drove Ben to the railroad station to take the train to Vancouver. The fire at the computer center took place on the nineteenth day of February, 1969, the same day Ben left home.

It had been going on for a long time before that, but that was the breaking point. That was when the children who were about to become adults said to their parents, "The power you wish to place in my hands can only lead me to murder!"

That was when they turned away in droves, became acid-heads, Jesus freaks, Hare Krishna freaks, itinerants, Weathermen, witch doctors, spiritual exiles. The daughters of dentists rummaging in garbage dumps for food, the sons of corporation lawyers living in abandoned buses, eating off food stamps, all of them saying that chosen poverty was more moral than mindless accumulation. That if you chose to be poor, you did not have to bear the guilt of being rich. That to be poor was to be holy.

That was when a whole band of children fell out of the world.

They were the unidentified casualties of the Vietnam war.

"Let's go home," my husband and I said to one another. "Let's go back to Sin City, let us live among our fellow sinners, for we are neither better than they, nor worse."

It was easier, back home. There were parades to march in, meetings to attend, leaflets to hand out. There was a label for people like us. We were "doves," and the other guys were "hawks." We were all Americans and we were having a ferocious family fight—over our inheritance.

I could grant myself an amnesty of the spirit because I was an adult. I possessed my own history. I could say to myself, "You, too, are a product of your times. You cannot be better than your generation. Millions of other Americans shared your fear, committed your sins. That is what it means to be human."

There was no way to turn the clock back, to retrace the steps, to relive, for Ben, the moment down in Washington, D.C., when the first contingent of a peace parade of half a million marched down Pennsylvania Avenue, led by soldiers of the United States Army in uniform; followed by veterans; followed by government employees, each of them wearing armbands to identify their agency—to save the FBI the trouble of picking them out from television cameras. No way to describe how it felt to march through the capital with a river of my fellow Americans who believed, in spite of all the evidence, that there was still something decent, something redeemable, something infinitely worth saving out of what we had become.

The sin which Ben had come here to expiate was the sin of being an American when all the world had reason to hate America. We had evaded the draft, but we had not escaped the war. In time, everyone who undertakes a great moral journey must confront the fact that the Devil is always the stowaway.

I was freezing up in the loft. I hobbled down the ladder, stiff in the hip as if I'd been in a wrestling match. It was oppressively still. The rain had stopped and Armstrong had vanished.

I stepped outdoors, looked up and down the empty road. There were no grand vistas, just a stretch of rutted dirt, a crowd of trees. Then a shadow fell on my shoulder and my heart pounded like a trip-hammer.

"It's nothing," I said to myself, wheeling around, seeing nobody behind me. But it was not nothing, because the shadow moved again. I saw it move out of the corner of my eye. No, I imagined it, out of my own fear. I walked slowly back to the Center and as I reached my hand out to open the door flap, the shadow climbed to the top of my shoulder. It was a large, brown beetle.

There was nothing else to do. Nowhere to go. No one to talk to. Nothing to see. I had come to the end of the road. So I climbed back into the loft and zipped myself back into the sleeping bag. Except that this time when Potlatch pursued me, I reached for her warm, black body and held her in my arms while I awaited eternity, or deliverance, whichever came first.

13

As he slid off the Power Wagon holding a drowsy Jimmy Finn in his arms, Ben looked like any tired, young family man who had put in a hard day at work and felt mighty pleased about it. Gilly and Ellis had stayed behind to spend the night on the Camp Nought float, guarding the shakes until the boat came by to pick them up. Diana, hurrying to get the children home to bed, asked me if she could bring her knitting over in the morning, before we left for Tibbett Lake. "Of course, Diana," I said.

Buddhi declined Ben's invitation to eat with us. He said he had a lot to do and couldn't spare the time. But before he ambled off into the dusk, he managed to say to me, in an aside, "You look as if you've been through a war. Are you all right?"

"I am now," I said. "But I don't respond very well to solitary confinement. I must be a compulsive communicator."

"Well, I wanted to tell you, you're doin' okay. Just keep biting through those wrappings!"

I was glad we did not have to spend another day at Capaswap Lake. Despite the proximity of the Finn family, Capaswap felt constraining to me, and it wasn't beautiful. In fact, in another year or two it was going to become a rural slum. Already a considerable quantity of industrial junk lay in a ravine near the facility, and the driveway of the Civic Center looked like a half-built service station, lined with oil drums and boxes of rags and all the greasy gear required to keep Ruby in working order.

Ben had already stowed his sleeping bag up in the loft when Diana came in, carrying her knitting in a pillow slip. "Listen," she repeated, "don't do it if you don't want to."

"But you aren't offending me by asking, Diana. I know how to do lots of other things beside knitting. I like to knit. It's nothing for a woman to be ashamed of."

She blushed behind her horn-rimmed glasses and said she wouldn't want me to think she was relating to me just as a sex or age stereotype.

I did not tell Diana that there was no secret to picking up the stitches she'd dropped all the way down near the sweater's ribbing. The only way to pick them up was to unravel the work down to the place she'd made the mistakes, and do it over. Or else accept the dropped stitches as evidence of human imperfection, and go on from there. Exactly as in life. I just patted her on the head once more, because I was the only mother who'd ever come here, and if anyone looked as if she could use a mother, it was Diana.

Now that I'd seen the other lakes on Proctor's Island, I understood why Ben had chosen Tibbett as his campsite. It was incredibly beautiful, a shining surface, lit along the shore with reflections of yellow green alder, and in the distance, above the black green mountain behind Ben's camp, the white peak of Mount Estero lording it over the mainland range. A trio of loons welcomed us as the canoe slipped out of the dark lagoon, giggling as if they thought it was a joke that I would think of going back to Ben's camp as "going home." And yet, I did. The woods around his little house were so healthy, so well-spaced, so tranquil. Everywhere I looked, from the garden to the Kiosk, there was a feeling of harmony, of fitness. Nothing mechanical obtruded. Everything looked natural, appropriate, in keeping with the spirit of the place. Even Gussie, with her bulging eyes and palpitating throat, who hopped out from under the workbench to greet me, did not hop away when I stooped to put a sliver of ham on the dirt floor before her.

It was easier now to talk to Ben. Having a sense of real accomplishment, he didn't need to be so defensive with me. We spent a couple of hours sitting in the sunshine down at the beach. There were gun shots back in the woods near Nootka Creek—Company guys, bored and depressed by the big silent forest, popped their pistols off at tin-can targets, just for something to do.

"I've done it myself, occasionally," Ben said. "You can get a little crazy up here, when everything's so quiet."

"How about drawing, Ben? Do you draw a lot?

"Not a whole lot, and not particularly well."

"Ben, may I see your notebook? It's been so many years since I've seen any of your work. I won't be critical . . ."

"That's what I'm afraid of," he said. "You'll start telling me about my beautiful mind, when it's only me, a punk, shooting off my mouth." But he did go back to get me the book.

It should have been called "Ben in Winter."

His images were sharp and stern. Double-faced men behind masks with double-hinged jaws. A wolf that looked like a sewing machine, and a sewing machine that looked like a wolf. Pages of chair designs, bathtub designs, house designs. Birds, large and small, flying, sitting in trees, walking, sleeping, birds reflected in the lake. Fish, singly or in quantity. A savagely funny portrait of Earl, and a gently indulgent portrait of a spaced-out Buddhi. Designs for rainhats made of cedar bark, extravagantly decorated and large as umbrellas. Drawings of drainpipes and plumbing connections, diagrams of geodesic dome frames, hexagrams from the *I Ching*. Fish counts, rainfall counts, water level counts. Weather observations. Recipes for hearty soups and powerful breads. Armstrong snoring on a doormat. A note: "March 22. Mom's birthday. Happy birthday, Mom!" And a beautiful drawing of a winged man flying toward the sun.

"Poems! You never told me you wrote poetry!"

> *You fast, moon.*
> *Faster than sun, moon.*
> *You bright, star!*
> *Corrugated and refracted*
> *Light, by my plastic, bright, star.*
> *You tick, watch.*
> *Trees have their own time, too, watch!*
>
> *Swan's honk clearer than mine*
> *But my song clearest of all!*
>
> *Echoes are as time warps*
> *Time warps are spirals*
> *My song spirals around Tibbett Lake.*

If you're making a living using your head
Not your hands
Unless you're doing something tricky
You'll never be on top of it.
There is also
Being reduced
To using your hands, and
This shows.

On another page,

A jet plane, perhaps a mile or two above the island's evening sky groans by, emitting two substantial poo-oooms, and I realize that to it, I am an uncharted undetermined speck on a radar screen which includes within its range the northern half of Oregon, east to the Cascades, north to Fairbanks as well as the coast, out to three hundred miles of North Pacific Ocean. If you think this makes me feel humble you would be making a big mistake.
Once one gets it out of their heads that it is actually possible to formulate, and I mean materialize, *the raw truth* . . . you know, *reality,* in a word form, then the whole works, everything you think say or do, falls into the hands of whoever you think you are.

"Ben, do you know that idea is known, in philosophy, as classical idealism?"

It's a cerebral world!
I've been so layed back
It's all I can do to keep the tree's energy
Contained in the heater
And my mind's eye
Directed
Outward.

On the next page, there was a large drawing of a man with a fish lying across his shoulder and a bird of prey standing on the fish, eating it. The man looked perplexed, helpless, caught on the horns of a moral dilemma. "Why doesn't he chase the bird away?" I asked Ben. "Because the bird has natural rights, too," he replied.

And then a diary entry which I recognized at once as a response to a letter Ben had just received from me. COMEBACKCOMEBACKCOMEBACKCOMEBACK! it said. And beneath it, encircled in red, it said

N O.

It was like reading a letter addressed to someone else. You never find anything to make you happy, reading someone else's letters. So I closed the book and gave it back to Ben.

Later, I made a picnic supper and brought it down to the beach while Ben built a fire on the sand in a circle of stones. He brought his wooden flute down, after we'd eaten, and played to the sunset, to the loons, and to the early peepers tuning up around the margin of the lake. He had no musical training, but his playing fit the forest—half bird call, half melody. Tall trees edged the pearly horizon, and the moon moved toward her fullness against the deepening sky.

A doe emerged from the thicket beyond the stump, not fifty yards from where we sat side by side on the log. She lifted her head above the underbrush, the firelight caught in her velvet eyes. She watched us in perfect silence for a long, long time before she bowed her firm, sculptured neck to drink. Watching her, Ben, too, seemed poised in perfect balance, on the very border between heaven and earth. He regarded the doe with wonderment, as if there were many lenses between him and the object of his observation. He had had that same look when he was an infant, as if he'd come into this life with a memory of another; and it would always be a secret where he kept his real self. Where are you going now, Ben? Into what vision? Would you ever take me with you to that place?

When the doe disappeared, he began to speak again. "I read this fantastic book, *Worlds in Collision,*" he said. And until the sunset was a purple smudge over the peaks of Vancouver Island, he talked about the creative imagination of a man who'd reconstructed a cosmic catastrophe, millenia past, and explained the floods, the droughts, the whole panoply of mankind's mythic past with his dazzling theories. Square scientists said Velikovsky was wrong. But what did it matter whether he was right or wrong? His ideas made stargazing such a terrific adventure.

Those stars were beginning to come out now, magnified and lengthened—"corrugated" was the word in Ben's poem—by their reflection on the lake. I'd never seen stars like this before. Not the dull glass chips of the thrift-shop suburban sky, but jewels. Real stars in a real sky, spinning through an open universe. Distant worlds swimming in their own cold fires. Could a man fall in love with the lights on a lake? I was prepared, at that moment, to believe it.

"Mom," he said after a while, "do you think a dog could commit suicide?"

"Why, no. That is, I can't imagine how."

I waited. And then Ben told me the true story of how he came to settle at Tibbett Lake:

"There was a guy up here by the name of Gary. A big revolutionary, chock full of well-advertised compassion. He had this puppy, a female Irish Setter who used to sleep with him in his sleeping bag. She was very highly bred, nervous, fawning, with long, red hair and big paws. Well, Gary got the September Twitch; needed broader horizons, greater freedom, wanted to go to California—without the dog. So he asked me to take her and I said no. He said she'd be a big money-maker if I bred her, but the idea made me sick. Besides, if she'd been bred with another setter, the pups would have jumped out of their skins.

"Finally he was going to leave the dog behind, so I agreed, and he signed the dog over to me. I liked having a dog for company, but she wasn't a good general all-around doggie dog, like Juno used to be; she was a nervous wreck, always under my feet, except when I went fishing. Then she'd go nuts, standing on the shore barking and yelping until I came back.

"I was in pretty bad shape myself at the time. I'd just lost a winter's supply of groceries when my skiff sank. They'd burned down the generator shack at Casin Point. I'd seen this place once and I liked it. So I collected everything I had, borrowed Dale's boat, and came over to Proctor's Island with the dog.

"It was early in November and it was very cold. We got to the float—my kayak was already there—and I was getting set for the last lap of the journey. But the dog was of two minds. She wanted to sit in my lap and be cuddled, but at the same time she refused to get into the kayak. Since my lap was in the kayak, she had to take the path around the lake.

"There's one place, a kind of cliff, where you have to climb a fair way up the mountain to get across. When the dog got to that point, I saw her groping along the edge, yapping and whining. I'd been yelling, 'Hey dog, come on now, dog!' so long that my voice was hoarse. It began to snow and it was nearly dark. By that time I was so disgusted with her that I left her to figure out how to cross the cliff by herself, and I paddled on down here, to the beach.

"Five minutes later, I stopped hearing her. Then I did hear a sound: a hoarse, desperate howl, and then nothing. And I knew that the dog was dead. I talked myself out of it, saying, 'Dogs don't kill themselves.' I couldn't believe a wolf got her. That night I was still expecting her to barrel into camp, when a wolf howled low. Vibrant. Close, conscious. And then I knew, for sure.

"That dog was . . . that dog must have represented, to me, a final, clinging presence, an interference with a sense of isolation that I had yet to—that I needed to—experience. When a wolf trotted along the lakeshore a few days later, came into my clearing and looked shocked to find me in his road, I felt like this—the wolf's—was the canine reality that suited my spirit. I never found the dog's bones or any trace of her."

It was the spirit of the wolf that I had seen on the wooden mask, lying now facedown in the long grass. It was the spirit of the wolf I'd seen on Ben's face when I wanted to call the pilot back, to cry out "Wait! Don't leave me here imprisoned in Ben's dream!" It was the spirit of a man trying to kill the softness in himself, to destroy the female within, cut it off and devour it like the starving Indian who consumed his own flesh.

It was his fall from innocence.

"I guess I have to prove something to myself," he said, after a long pause.

"What is it that you have to prove, Ben?"

"Maybe that my life is worth saving, that I'm worth

the effort it takes to keep myself alive. When nobody's leaning on you, nobody's telling you what to do . . . if you let go, nobody's going to miss you, either. . . ."

"But you've already proven that you can survive the wilderness, that you can manage alone. Do you have to go on proving it, forever? Don't you see, you can never become a whole human being, living apart from other people? Never learn to cope with the good and the evil that's in you, and in everybody else, unless you're part of a human society?"

"I've got no choice," he said in a very low voice. "I've got no cash, and I've got no company. And because I don't have them, can't have them, I've said I didn't want them. But it's not true. It was never true. I wish I had money. I wish I did have company."

14

It had taken all this time to bite-through-the-wrappings. If nothing else, my coming here had forced Ben to admit to a few home truths. From now on, he would not talk to me, of cosmic energy when he really meant cold cash. He would not speak of inner space when he really meant stark loneliness.

I'd have been glad to sit and talk until it was time to climb into the canoe and wave a blanket at a passing plane. But we had to go back to Capaswap Lake because the shakes had not been picked up, after all. Ellis came by to tell us so.

"Cripes!" Ben said mildly, as if it were a matter of limited consequence to him.

"A lost cause!" I thought, mentally throwing up my hands. "So what does it matter if he starves this summer? He can always live on clams, mushrooms, plantain. This soil is so rich and so on and so forth."

Although Ellis did not say so, and was probably too young even to suspect it, I assumed that the shipper he had contacted had had second thoughts, wondered if he was going to get paid for his trouble. This time Dale was taking charge of the arrangements, which he should have done in the first place. He would have enough sense to involve Ray Beame, the lighthouse keeper, in the contact. Even if Ray only introduced Dale on the telephone it would give his order substance and authority. Put the stamp of government approval on the negotiation. But how would any of these children know this? All they knew was that the shakes weighed tons, and that it was a hard job moving them off the float again, hiding them in the forest. Of course we would go back to help finish the job.

We put off our departure for Capaswap until late afternoon. Ben's mountains made shiny black shadows on Tibbett Lake when we set out for the second shake move. As he predicted, the wind shifted to a strong westerly blow, which twisted my oar and carried it high above the choppy surface of the water. It took a firm grip to slice into it sideways and thrust deep for a long stroke. As we neared Buddhi's island, I felt a change in our direction and thought Ben was taking us into its lee to reduce the force of the wind. I did not see Buddhi standing on a lichen-covered cliff, for the sun was behind the island, shining like polished silver, and Buddhi was scarcely visible against the density of his backdrop.

He and Ben greeted one another with the raven cry, but we did not enter his little harbor. "We're moving the shakes back to Camp Nought," Ben said.

"I can't come this time," Buddhi replied with sweet

regret. "Very important cosmic event coming up. An eclipse of the full moon, and it falls on Buddha's birthday."

It went without saying that Buddhi's religious observances took precedence over practical matters. Ben made light of the purpose of our voyage, noting instead the date and time of the eclipse and wishing his friend a great spiritual experience.

"I've got a lot to do to get ready," Buddhi said. "Cutting salal for a fire." Indeed, I noticed that his incense burner was already on a rock beside the shore, along with a transistor radio.

We crossed the lake in record-breaking time, with Ben making precise calculations of the variations in wind resistance, relative distances, and manpower. "It's almost twice as fast when you're paddling, too," he said.

Instead of heading for the Civic Center, we took a right fork onto the new road around Capaswap. It was a dusty, raw cut, with trucks and caterpillar tractors parked along the side. A little distance beyond the churned-up creek bed, a stand of recently-felled timber opened up a long view down Capaswap Lake. A mass of purple clouds hung low over the surrounding hills, ragged with golden glory. We kept to the road for a quarter of a mile, then entered the twilight forest that led to Dale's house. It was a spirit world, a fairy-tale wood, a black immensity of trees, lance-tipped and upward-thrusting far beyond human range. Blue green ferns sprouted from the soil and a hemlock a yard thick grew out of the prone body of its ancestor, reaching around the fallen form, fastening itself and its progenitor to earth with roots like pinions. As we climbed over rocks and broke through underbrush, the setting sun hurled one last golden beam through the trees, awakening

a terrible longing in me for the dream-home of my childhood. As the last of the daylight dimmed, someone up
ahead lit a lamp. The dream-home of my childhood materialized. It was Dale's place.

It took a bottle of wine and a good dinner to diminish
the magic that surrounded this dwelling. Even when
Jimmy leaned against my knee and poked at my chest to see
if all that upholstery was real, it was hard to forget the
primeval drama of the darkness outside. It was Diana
who'd lit the evening lamp that made the three, intercon-
nected geodesic domes "home." Dale added fresh wood to
an open-fronted Franklin stove and served up a well-
cooked stew, simmered on a regulation stove and served in
bowls that once belonged to a matching set. Which was
real, I kept asking myself, what was outside or what was
inside?

Diana was grateful for the job I'd done on her knitting.
She put out a lot, taking responsibility for Dale's children.
She must wonder, in the dark of night, I thought, whether
she was ever likely to have her effort repaid. For Dale was
not an easy-going or protective man. Apart from his relationship with his children, he seemed hollow, as if something important were missing within him. He'd studied for
the priesthood and left before taking orders, to blow a
sudden inheritance on the making of a documentary film
about the Eskimos. There was a lot of photographic equipment in the middle section of the house, but it looked
neglected and disused.

All my efforts to connect with Dale seemed to miss
their mark. If I said the forest was full of night spirits, he
said it was just such and so many running-board-feet of
timber. If I asked about the price of cedar shakes, he de-

plored the individualistic, dog-eat-dog spirit of a local population that made the organization of militant cooperatives impossible. "The old Wobbly spirit's dead—bought off by welfare. Sad!" he said.

There was a self-deprecating, mock-martyrdom in his tone, as if he were saying "If other people had courage, took risks—like me—we could get something done!" But at the same time shrugging off responsibility. "How can we possibly accomplish anything here, when all the odds are stacked against us?"

Years ago, I'd have described Dale as a petit-bourgeois anarchist. Even assuming that what he would have liked to accomplish was entirely in keeping with the public weal, I was tempted to say, "If you didn't go about everything so ass-backwards, you might find out!" But I didn't.

Mostly because Ben was there, and Ben was very serious. He said it was a real opportunity for all of them that I was here, because I was the only one who had any experience, any perspective about what was going on. Why, he asked me, did I really think that the Company and the government were opposed to homesteaders living on Proctor's Island, when it was so obvious that the forests needed the attention and the hand-labor of people who cared about them?

"I guess because machines are more predictable than people. They don't have opinions. You don't have to bury them when they die. Even the Cosmic Copulator doesn't produce children who eventually need schools, health services, roads . . . all that."

And Dale said, "What you've got here, Ben, is a very vulnerable natural resource standing around waiting to be harvested. It brings out the primitive impulse in people.

They'll make a wasteland of it yet. Smokey the Bear can't stand up to the cost accountants. We're just living on the system's inefficiency . . . an oversight . . . but it's just a matter of time before . . ."

"Oh, Dale!" cried Diana, "You don't really believe that, do you?"

"Well, we can hold them off for a while. Maybe for years. Give them a good run for their money. But . . ." And he shrugged.

"Swen's bringing along the new contract, isn't he?" Ben broke in.

"Yeah. And he tagged the rest of the shakes before we took them back off the float. Say, we got another shipper. Can you get going at five o'clock tomorrow morning? According to the Tide Book . . ." And they were off again and running. There was still no plan for storing the shakes in Vancouver while someone went hunting for a customer, but it was *infra dig* to mention it.

"Did you guys know there's going to be an eclipse of the full moon?" Ben said.

"Will it be auspicious for moving the shakes?" Diana inquired.

While Dale took us across the lake to the Civic Center in his canoe, he told a story about meeting two Company men—one right after the other—on the new road the day before. "It was interesting," he said, "because both of them were talking about the same set of facts, but one of them was a working stiff on a motorcycle and the other was a supervisor in a truck. The first guy was a robot. We had an info-data-swap: 'Can't do this, gotta do that, how many, when did such and such, as soon as, and certainly no later than . . .' He never took his hands off the handlebars. Two minutes later, the supervisor comes over, stands with his hands in his pockets, and tells me the exact same set of facts, only every sentence begins with 'So I told that jerk to . . .' and, 'If he thought I was going to . . .' Like the job was a diplomatic negotiation! He must have had a couple of years of college, to know that the facts could be altered, depending on who you were . . .''

Whatever Dale was or was not, I decided he certainly was not a fool.

I had every intention of going along on the trip to Camp Nought, even if it meant getting up at five o'clock in the morning. But when Dale and Diana arrived at the Center and said, "Time to get up!" I rolled to the edge of the loft and said, "Where are the children?"

Diana giggled. "We left them alone—to wrestle with the bears!"

I thought about that while Ben got up and made a pot of tea. Gilly and Ellis staggered over, still half-asleep, from the house next door.

"No kidding, Di. Where are the children?" I said again.

"They're at home, sleeping. I left their breakfast on the table. We told them they could come over here whenever they got up, and they could stay here with you until we got back. That is, unless you'd rather not. If you'd rather not, they can just . . . well, stay here by themselves and play."

"They'll come over in a canoe?"

"Oh, no, the canoe's on this side. They'll walk around on the road. They always walk. Would you mind?"

"Well, no, I wouldn't mind at all. That's good. Very

good. So I don't have to get up. Good night!" And rolling
back into my nylon cocoon, I did not even hear the Power
Wagon making her cacophonous departure down the road
to Camp Nought.

That wonderful second sleep! That deep plunge into
the unconscious! I sank into it with a sense of utter aban-
don, for it was not rest I required at five o'clock in the
morning, but a wild adventure of the mind. I dreamed that
fire engines were clanging down my street, that someone
had set fire to the grass behind my house, that the flames
were licking toward the big pine trees. I dreamed that the
air raid siren was wailing from the roof of the fire station.

I was not dreaming. The air raid siren on the roof of
the fire station *was* wailing. But I was on Proctor's Island,
and there were no fire engines and no air raid sirens here.
Yet, a lacerating howl curled up from the earth on the other
side of the plastic wall. A song shaped like a corkscrew,
rising directly out of the ground beneath the loft. I knew
who was singing. It was the Wolf.

I reached three fingers out of the sleeping bag and
drew the hoodstring tight, so that only my nostrils were in
contact with the outer air. The noise of the bunching nylon
was deafening.

There was a third howl, and a fourth, ranging up and
down the scale in a bone-chilling sequence.

I knew precisely where my duty lay. I ought to have
leaped out of the loft, jumped into the canoe, paddled to the
other side of Capaswap Lake, snatched those innocent children out of their beds and carried them—somewhere, anywhere—to safety. A fifth howl, and my blood congealed. If
they were my children, what would I do? If they were my
children I would never have left them alone. Yet I was

serving *in loco parentis.* What if a wolf attacked Astri? No, everybody here insisted that wolves did not attack humans. But how about children?

Besides, I comforted myself that Astri and Jimmy knew more about wolves than I did. Wolves were part of their circumstance. If I reacted with panic, it would disable them for the life they had to lead.

There was a long silence. I lifted my head carefully, just far enough to peep over the edge of the loft. Potlatch lay prone beside the Airtight, dead of heart failure. If I lifted my head any farther, I would see a huge gray animal sitting in the driveway watching me through green eyes that were so clear I would see all the way back into its stomach. But the wolf was not on the road, for he sang once more, right beneath the loft.

"Be *rational!*" I told myself as I lay motionless in a puddle of sweat. "*Pray!*"

When the wolf sang again, the sound came from a distance, perhaps near Scott Woriaki's string and plastic house. If it was the same wolf, he was faster than the speed of light. If it was a second wolf, and they were closing in . . .

If it was the same wolf, he was already closer to the children than he was to me. Even if I'd managed to find the path through the woods, even if I'd found Dale's canoe, even if I'd paddled it across the lake without turning it over, even if I'd found Dale's house, even if I could have frightened off a hungry wolf with a stick, the wolf would have known my intentions, would have read my mind on an updraft, and would have gotten to the children ahead of me. Everybody knows how intelligent wolves are. And suppose, while I was paddling across the lake, the children had already gotten out of bed and started running around the edge of the lake? And ran smack into the second wolf?

One last time the song of the wolf rose on the morning air, but this time the sound was so distant I could scarcely hear it. He was on his way back to his lair on the mountain behind Ben's camp. He was just telephoning his family long-distance to say, "Yes, she's still around".

The children were perfectly safe and, if I did not tell them, they would have no way of knowing I'd betrayed them. Liberal that I am, I'd paid my debt by torturing my conscience on their behalf. But my action demonstrated just what Darwin observed a hundred years ago: that self-preservation was then, and is now, the first law of nature.

There was no wind. Save for the crackle of wood in the Airtight, and the thrumming of mice, the air was as noiseless as sunlight. Potlatch snoozed on beside the stove, signaling by the twitch of her tail that she was still alive and well. Armstrong materialized in the driveway after awhile and whined, looking downcast, as if to say "I thought Ellis would surely be back by now." Elbow after elbow, he let himself down onto the driveway and rested his muzzle on the tips of his paws.

"If the animals are bored, the wolf must have gone for good," I thought, and eased myself out of the loft to bathe and dress. It was a little after nine o'clock, and I prowled around the Center as quietly as possible, so as not to miss the first gay shouts of the children as they flip-flopped down the road.

Meanwhile, the sun was warming up the Center. A little breeze rattled the plastic walls and rustled the branches of the trees in the ribbon of woods that lay between the house and the lakeshore. There was a sudden, loud splash in the lake, quite possibly a bear or a cougar or an honest-to-God beaver: a once-in-a-lifetime opportunity to steal up on a genuine creature of the wilds, unseen. But I got up slowly from the armchair and closed the plastic door flap. Then there was a sharp pop, like gunshot, and I thought "Please God, whatever it is, just don't let it walk past me on the road!" Then a second shot rang out, but this time I saw that it was the sun-warmed expansion of an oil drum out in the driveway. See how foolish I was? Getting all upset over natural phenomena? By ten o'clock I could not keep myself inside the Center any longer, so I walked outside, hoping to see the children running around the bend in the road.

The sun was shining cheerfully. A few birds sang. Fluffy little clouds floated across the sky. Potlatch and Armstrong had both disappeared. "Nothing bad can happen on such a pretty day," I said to myself. And sat down to watch the minute hand of my antique watch crawl around its face.

It was half-past eleven when I heard Astri's clear little voice calling "Jimmmmmmeeeeee!" I dashed out into the road. They were gamboling toward me with their jackets open, their hair mussed, their cheeks flushed, floppy-footed and high on sensation.

"Guess what! Guess what!" Astri squeaked. "We just seen the *biggest fucking wolf tracks ever!*"

"At the turn of the road!" said Jimmy.

I hugged them both to my chest and tried to restrain a sob.

"What did you *do?* What are you supposed to do?"

"Whatdya mean," Astri said, drawing away from me.

"We didn't see the *wolf,* we just seen the *tracks!*"

"No," Jimmy corrected her, "what she means is, you're supposed to stay in the house and be quiet . . . else they'll come inside and eat you all *op!*"

"That's what I did," I said, and turned back to the Center to get a Kleenex.

Jimmy trailed in after me, maybe hoping for a handout of raisins.

"Do you know what?" he inquired in a tone that made it clear he was about to offer me the ultimate in astonishment. "One time I read a book about a place where there was *no animals!*"

They were splendid company and talked incessantly, both to me and to one another. Astri made up in competence what she lacked, with Jimmy, in seniority. "I'm four," she announced, holding up four fingers with some difficulty. "Your jacket's too big for you."

"I know," I replied. "I bought it too big on purpose, because I'm going to give it to Ben when I go back home."

This idea required work. It was funny to her that clothing could be passed along because it was too big. Likely everything she ever owned came down to her from Jimmy because it was too small.

She rummaged among the containers under the loft and found two pieces of chalk. She gave the shorter piece to Jimmy and wrote ASTRI on the floor. "I write like Diana," she said. "I dry myself like Diana, too!" And she bowed out her short little legs and passed an imaginary towel back and forth between them.

"You're not s'posed to write on Ben's floor," Jimmy said as he wrote JIMMY next to her name.

"It's not Ben's floor. It's the Cicenter's floor."

"Ben built it! Know what? I'm going to school pretty soon."

"How will you do that, Jimmy? There isn't a school on Proctor's Island. Will you go by boat?"

"I dunno, but I'm going."

Whereupon Astri handed me her piece of chalk and said, "This is for you to keep. It's very smooth."

Jimmy suggested that we all walk down to Camp Nought, and laughed when I wondered if five miles wasn't too far. "We allus walk it," he said, puzzled that I did not know that the road was the block, the movies, school, radio, and television, all rolled into one. "Swen brings me bubble gum," Astri boasted. "He says it's OK to drop the papers on the road, he'll bury 'em with his cat' tractor."

"Swen allus asks *me* to catch him some *frogs* for his dinner!" said Jimmy. And they both pretended to puke.

Jimmy left the road frequently. He ran up and down a series of sand piles, yelling, "Yah! Yah! Lookit me!" He disappeared into a meadow to pick some flowers for me, some fiddlehead ferns for Ben, and a pocketful of stones for himself, to throw at trees. On the way, he lost his new sweater and mourned his misfortune at length.

Complacently, Astri assured him they would find the sweater on the way back. "You lose everything," she said. She did not waste her energy on extravagant excursions. She kept to the road, varying the journey by altering her own persona. She trailed a large, leafy branch behind herself for a while, wiggling her hips. Then she took off her raincoat and put it on back to front. Then she threaded one arm through both sleeves and carried her coat as if it were hung on a walking washline. She collected stones from a little rivulet that trickled at the border of the road, then paused and painstakingly undid the safety pin that held her jeans together at the waist. Bare-bottomed and ravishing, she crouched and peed. Fifty paces farther on, she knelt to drink from the same little rivulet. "Astri!" I cried. "You just peed in that water!" "It's OK," she said, wiping her mouth with the back of her little, brown hand, "If it's running, you can drink it."

With her intense absorption in immediate detail, it was not to be wondered that it was Astri who noticed Ben's hunting knife lying on the road. "He's going to be so mad at hisself that he lost it! He's going to be so glad at me that I found it!"

"I wisht it was me that found it," Jimmy said with honest sorrow. "Ben taught me how to tie my shoelaces."

Astri rode her victory over her brother a step farther. "One time me and Dale were hunting, I seen a *wolf!* It was all *silver!*" She drew her breath in sharply, spreading her fingers wide to dramatize the shock of encounter.

"I never even *seen* a wolf," Jimmy said, awash in self-pity.

Their talk was so diverting, I scarcely noticed the road or the time it took to get to the end of it. For the last mile or so, they seemed to need an adult hand to hold. I loved the feeling of the three of us walking together, attached, but their weight pulled on my old bursitis. I explained that I couldn't hold their hands and walk at the same time. Could they slip a finger through a belt loop, or into the pocket of my jeans, instead? "Oh, sure!" they said, glad to oblige. But seconds later each of them reached for my hand again, in the most intuitive and the most moving of all human gestures; and thus we walked all the way to the border of the sea.

It always is an astonishment to come upon the sea. It is always the first time, for me, as if the ocean were a gift which someone thought to give me only a moment before. Standing at the end of the road, I could believe that the broad, blue ribbon of water opened right into the great Pacific; that the whales were on their way across from China, to play. "Everything is possible!" the ocean always said to me.

"Halllloooo!" the children cried, breaking from my side in a wild, downhill dash into the arms of their family and their familiars. "Haloooo!" the open-armed harbor cried to me. "Haloooo!" rebounded against the rocks, a rising call of greeting from the toilers by the sea.

"I lost my sweater!" cried Jimmy.

"I found your knife!" cried Astri.

Camp Nought was an abandoned logging camp like the Ruins, with weathered shacks and verdant beach grass and wild flowers blooming in the rusted frame of an overturned truck. The Power Wagon was parked at a steep tilt, with her back wheels at the very bottom of the pebbly beach. Diana was dragging a bundle of shakes from the flatbed, staggering to the water's edge, and dropping the bundle into the shallows. Gilly stood astride two wet rocks, dodged the splash, and poled the shakes out to the float. Ellis crouched at the edge of the float, hauling the bundles up out of the water before they bobbed past beyond his reach. Ben stood knee-deep in the water, between the float and the rocks, bearing down on a long plank, and Dale was hurrying across the rocks carrying a great loop of rusty iron cable over his shoulder.

I took a balcony seat at the top of the rocks, from which to survey the theater of operations. Dale followed my eyes

to the tugs plying Dyer Strait, southward bound, each of
them towing a long string of timber-laden barges. "They're
working on Sunday to beat the strike deadline," he said.

"Is it Sunday already?" I said.

The main channel seemed to be about five miles from
the shore of Proctor's Island, close to the coast of the next
island south. Somewhere among the low, blue hills on the
horizon was Casin Point, where Ben used to live. A red-
and-white-striped lighthouse stood at a tip of land jutting
out from Vancouver Island, looking tiny and magical in the
afternoon haze.

I watched Dale wind the heavy cable around a rock.
"The float's caught down there," he said, "and the tide's
running out. We've got to lift it off, before the tide goes out
much farther." The float was a beat-up parallelogram of
mammoth logs, heavy enough to hold a couple of Mack
trucks; I couldn't imagine how Dale and Ben thought there
was a chance of lifting it by any system of leverage. But
they'd looked for the solution in the problem, and found it.
If one big wave had carried the float over the rock, another
big wave might lift it off. The thing was to wait until the
wash from one of those coastal steamers, five miles away,
hit the shore of Proctor's Island. By adding their own
power to the sea's, they only needed to choose exactly the
right moment to act.

Ben found the best spot under the float to insert his
lever, Dale and Ellis got a firm hold on the cable, and when
the wash came rolling toward the rock, Dale cried, "Here
she comes! Ready, set, *lift!*" And with a great surge the float
rode over the rock and slid back, free, on the heaving water.

"You can do anything you want to do!" I thought, of
Ben. "Anything."

While Jimmy roamed the beach in search of purple crabs, Astri played in half of an old rowboat, a bit of sea wrack bleaching near my rock roost. Suddenly she jumped up and, holding her hand away from herself as if it did not belong to the rest of her body, cried, "I got a splinter! I got a big splinter!" And she made straight for Ben. Forehead to forehead they knelt on the rock, studying her outstretched hand. "I've got to use the sharpest thing to take it out," Ben said. "It won't hurt so much if it's sharp. Okay with you? I'll use the flat side of my knife."

She nodded solemnly, never taking her eyes off her finger, all her tension in the torque of her body. "Ben," I heard her ask as he pressed the knife against the sliver, "If you were *awful* hungry, could you eat yourself?"

"Uh-huh," he replied. "Indians used to, sometimes."

"Oh," she said.

When he drew the splinter out, Ben sucked the blood from her finger and spat it out, told her to wash her hand well in the salt water. "It'll sting a little, but you've got to get it clean." A few minutes later, Astri was back in the rowboat, playing, and I heard her say to herself once more, "Oh."

A good while before the last of the shakes reached the float, Gilly called it quits. She looked as if she'd spent the last of her energy hours ago and was just hanging in for the sake of appearances. She climbed wearily onto the rocks and rolled herself a cigarette, her arms hanging loosely over her knees. But Diana stuck it out to the very last. Before she climbed up beside Gilly, she fetched a pencil and a small pad of paper from the truck. She was very thin, fragile, and a blue vein pulsed near the base of her neck. Each bundle of shakes she'd carried must have weighed nearly as much as she did. Bracing the pad against her knees she covered the paper with calculations, enclosing each group of figures with a penciled square. "If we get such and such for the shakes," she announced, "you and Ellis will get so and so much and Ben will . . . But if we only get . . ." The net profit to the Finn family would have equaled two months' rent on an apartment in a medium-sized city, and Ben's share might cover a six-week supply of groceries.

I knew what they needed of me, and it wasn't harsh, practical reality. What they needed now was for their labor to be sanctified, to transcend the cash that it would bring. I realized suddenly that it was not for Swen's sake that they'd wanted to load up the shakes before their meeting, but for mine. Because it was nearly time for me to go and they wanted me to see, to know, they wanted me to believe in them, because I was history. I was the larger context, the seeing eye, the continuity with the past in which they had to feel their rootedness if they were ever to succeed. It wasn't only Ben who needed the touch of my hand, the pronouncement, the imprimatur of my approval—it was all of them. Even Dale.

"Bravo! you all," I said, climbing down to sit beside them on the seaweed-fringed rock. "Well done."

They passed a smoke around, one to another, offered me a drag. Squinting through the smoke, I counted eight squat, sturdy pillars of bundled shakes, oblong cubes of sliced cedar, two-by-two-by-three, each bound with a black steel strap, and tagged and stamped, glowing orange in the afternoon sun. Each one was a miracle of manufacture, perseverance, imagination, muscle-power, idealism, cooperative endeavor. Each of them represented a journey from dream to reality, the overcoming of doubt, the triumph over lassitude, the assertion of a will to live, to cope with necessity, to discover a new and better way to survive in an unreasonable world.

"Do you know what you've accomplished out there?" I said to all of them, but mostly to Ben. "You've created a marketable commodity—out of cosmic energy!"

15

It was raining cats and dogs. Water coursed down the plastic walls of the Civic Center like the Monday morning blues.

If I could have left with the vision of those eight golden pillars of saleable shakes shining in my mind, I could have carried the notion home that in a week, or two, or three, Ben would have the cash with which to buy the next season's supply of food, that he would be a little bit ahead in his contest for survival. By the end of the coming summer there might be letters describing other schemes, like the launching of a cedar craft for a coastal journey to Alaska. By winter, when snow would pile in curving drifts in the corners of my heated windows, perhaps I would have found some way not to wonder if he had enough energy to keep a fire going in the Airtight, and his mind's eye directed outward.

But there was still the meeting.

The membership of the Coastal Environment Cooperative would not be present in overwhelming numbers. Ellis had stayed at Camp Nought with the shakes and planned to go down to Vancouver on the boat to supervise their storage—it was not yet settled where—and try to sell them. Buddhi was preoccupied with his religious observations. MaryLou and Dunc had retired to nurse their frazzled nerves. Scott Woriaki had not yet arrived. Which left Dale and Diana, Ben and Gilly—and me.

Nevertheless, Diana had written out an eight-point agenda on a blackboard, which she propped on a straight-backed chair in the middle of the floor of the Civic Center. Ben and I hurried through breakfast, washed all the tea mugs, emptied the ashtrays, swept the floor with the broom stub, loaded up the box with firewood, and arranged half a dozen chairs borrowed from the other houses in a half-circle, saving the slope-backed armchair for Swen.

I told Ben about the wolf who had visited me, and he grinned.

"I guess it sounds funny to you," I said, "but it didn't feel so funny to me."

"I know, Mom," he said, apologetically. "I didn't mean to . . . but I guess I ought to tell you. It was probably Armstrong. He's half-wolf, you know. He carries on like that when he thinks Ellis has gone away and left him forever. Did he sound like this?" And he sang the same corkscrew song my wolf had sung the day before. It was a good thing for Armstrong that he wasn't there, else I might have given him a good, swift kick.

Overhead, a single-motor plane was coming down. "That's Swen! Right on time!" Ben said, lifting the lid of the Airtight with the wooden handle I'd made for him and throwing in a fresh load of wood. He ran down the path to the lakeshore and returned a minute later. "The plane's gone over to Dale's landing! Come on, let's go!"

I buttoned myself into my rain jacket and slogged down the muddy road, doing my best to keep up with Ben. The white seaplane was pulled up close to Dale's wharf, an alien and obtrusive shape against the ragged, scudding surface of the lake. The arbitrary change in arrangements did not bode well for the Company's intentions. It implied a decision to deal with Dale as an individual, rather than as the president of the organization. Still, it was realistic.

The children intercepted us on the road. "They're here!" Astri cried in her piercing voice. "Diana says to come quick!"

"There's four of 'em!" cried Jimmy, "and they've all got short hair!"

"Four!" echoed Astri.

The woods behind Dale's house looked intensely domestic in the morning light. A huge pile of sawdust lay beside his workbench. Wheelbarrows and bags of cement stood on a platform where a bathtub of fieldstone was taking shape. Nearby, there was a facility shielded with plastic and mounted on a high platform, and big water drums and a gas tank attached to the house. Children's toys were scattered among the tools, and the storage space beneath the floor of the house was crowded with commodities in bulk containers. In spite of the looseness of the housekeeping, it was a family dwelling, a going concern—no fly-by-night operation, but a well-fixed establishment organized and maintained by someone with a will to be reckoned with.

No introductions were made when Ben and I entered

the house. The four strangers scarcely looked up to acknowledge our arrival. Ben motioned me to sit on an overturned nail keg. He took up a post against the doorframe,
opposite Dale, who stood beside the Franklin stove con-
ducting the meeting with his eyes. The Company men
were sitting around the low coffee table, Gilly and Diana
completing the semicircle. I smelled slaughter.

"... meant to bring along a slide show, to let you
people see the whole scope of the Company's operations,"
a sporty-looking young man in a white, saddle-stitched
sport jacket was saying, "... so you'd understand what
we're trying to accomplish here ..."

He was interrupted by a tense-looking man in steel-
rimmed glasses who slipped a pencil through his fingers,
hitting it against a brown portfolio on his knees, first with
the point and then with the eraser: "You realize the cost to
the company every time there's a fire? We've got to take
five, six men off the job, put them on firefighting. That costs
a lot of money, you know."

"But we're not the ones who start fires, Mr. Winlaw,"
Diana said.

The man continued as if he had not heard what she
said. "Trouble is, when you've got people living in here,
you can't *control* them. You can't control a place where
there's people. We've got a very big investment to protect
up here. You get a couple of hunters, they shoot up the
equipment, strip the trucks . . . it costs like the devil!"

"Yes, but you're not talking about *us*," Dale said
blandly, and I thought of the Cosmic Copulator.

The older man, the one sitting closest to the door,
exchanged a quick glance with Ben, who smiled with constraint, as if to say "We do know one another, don't we? We

don't have to pretend we're someone else, just because those other guys are here, do we?"

"Things have changed a lot since I started with the Company," Swen Mohring said. He had a kind of back-country drawl, but he sounded very tired. "What you don't understand, Finn, is that we've got to meet international competition. Them Japs and Chinks are out to undercut our prices. Trouble with thinning is, it costs too much. Drives up the price. People got to be able to buy the product. What'll folks do if they can't afford to buy? We'll get drove right out of the market!"

Diana spoke. "You're paying five dollars an hour down on Quadra, Swen. How do you expect us to do thinning for five dollars a day?"

"They got good equipment on Quadra. They're efficient. They turn in a day's work. Them guys work thirteen hours a day," he said with a referred glance toward young Mr. Winlaw, who was still playing with the pencil. Swen was thinking of his job.

Public-relations-in-the-saddle-stitched-jacket took up the cudgels. "You just don't get the whole picture," he repeated, addressing himself to Dale. "It's not just you people we got to worry about. Don't you think we aren't getting plenty of flak from the tourist people? They want us to leave a front across from their damned hotels—lose thousands of running feet of timber, just so the tourists don't have to see a slash. Just to work what's out of sight. Why, all they have to do is put up a goddamn lodge and they'll shut the whole place down!"

"It don't make no difference, from five miles away, so long as it looks green . . ." the pencil player said.

"And how long does it take, generally speaking, for it

to turn green again?" I asked, addressing my question to Swen.

He looked acutely embarrassed, as if I had done something outrageous and unthinkable to enter the discussion.

"Couple of years," he said, blushing to the tips of his long, pendulous earlobes. "Well, maybe five, ten, depending . . ."

The silent man sitting next to Gilly shuffled his feet and cleared his throat. He looked pale and haggard. Most of the time he stared at his knees, as if his eyes might go bad from looking around this haphazard household.

The young man who had not been able to bring along the slide show leaned forward, putting a severe strain on his trousers. "Country can't run without timber. You people 'way out here, you don't see the whole picture. Competition's killing us. Now . . . about this contract." He picked up a folded paper lying on the coffee table and said, "From now on, you can submit sealed bids for the thinning, just like everybody else. And this . . ." He tore the paper in two, leaving the sound standing by itself in the middle of the room. "This old contract's canceled . . . just as you asked. Swen? Did you want to . . ."

"Waaall," Swen said, laboring to his feet as if he was feeling his age, "no need to . . . right now. That there young feller's gotta get a move on." And he nodded toward the pale young man across the table. "Pretty pricey, charterin' a plane by the hour. Ay-ah! Costs a-plenty!" he said to no one in particular, since everyone was moving, turning, shifting, easing toward the door. His eyes skidded past me. He stepped back to let the three younger men precede him out of the house, waited for Dale to join him. Together they filed down the path toward the plane, whose outspread wings were visible through the dripping trees.

"Those bastards!" Diana said. "Acting as if they owned the place!" And she buried her head in her folded arms.

"They do!" said Gilly, hunched forward, elbows on knees, rolling a cigarette. "Who the hell wants to spend thirteen hours a day cutting down trees? All that stink, that noise. You might as well go work in a factory in Fat City. It doesn't make any sense! That's not what we're here for, to cut down trees . . ."

Diana stared at the floor. "Swen's right," she said. "If they can't meet the competition, they'll go out of business. People need what they make. I want to be able to buy . . . we can't exist without them . . ."

"But that's not true!" Ben protested. "The thing is, we've got to have as little to do with them as possible. You can't let yourself get sucked into their lousy system. There's no way to beat them on their own ground. Our weakness is our strength. We've got to play it cool. Once you start thinking like they do, you're cooked. We'd lose everything!"

Diana's eyes, sunken with fatigue, brimmed with tears.

"Who's *us?* Ben? Who've we got?"

"As long as there are even two of us," Ben said staunchly, "the cooperative is viable. Even one of us can survive. I've proven that myself. One person can last here three—even four—months alone!"

We heard the motor starting up, whirring louder and louder until, with a heavy snore, it ripped across the lake and droned off into the sky. Dale came back into the house. His face was like a cinder.

He lit a cigarette in silence, then poured coffee for everyone.

"What's that?" Diana asked as he leaned over the table, exposing the corner of a white envelope in the inner pocket of his jacket.

He drew deeply on the cigarette, let the smoke out slowly through his nostrils.

Dale looked at me and tried to smile. "Swen said he didn't want to give it to me . . . in front of . . . you. It's an eviction notice."

I was afraid to meet Ben's eyes. Surely he knew that my wish for him had just come true. Except I wasn't so sure any more. Some old ember of defiance flared in me, struggling for life. Every generation needed a vision, had to try to remake the world. These were good people—maybe the best and the bravest of their generation. Putting their lives on the line for what they believed. Why couldn't they go on together, learning, growing, taking care of the forests, living happily ever after? Who were those walking cash registers to lord it over them, to exploit them, to put them off the land?

"When? Is it legal? How long? Who signed it?" the others asked, crowding around Dale to read the notice.

"We'll contest it," Dale said, "but it's going to take a lot of talking. It's not a government action. I don't think they've got legal grounds. We don't have a contract for thinning, but we've still got the timber lease. That's what counts." His dark face was deeply furrowed but he held his head up, staring out of the plastic window into space.

For a moment I heard the old marching songs again.

"You know what impressed me most?" I said. "How scared they all were, of all of you. That they had to send three men and a pilot for the kiss-off . . ."

Ben looked at me searchingly, as if he'd just been shaken awake from a long dream.

"What the hell do *they* have to be afraid of," Diana demanded.

"Why, that you're real people. Not just a faceless bunch of hippies. That each and every one of you has more guts in your little finger than any one of them. You're a living demonstration that you can survive outside the system. Look around! Nothing's locked up. Counted. Insured. Zoned. Everything's out in the open. Hanging loose. Yet it's a real home. This is a real family. Maybe it's not a regulation house, but you live in it. You're free. That's not only frightening to square people, it's absolutely subversive!"

"Right *on!*" cried Gilly, raising a fist in salute.

"You don't have to be exploited. You don't have to be inefficient. There's no special virtue in letting them take advantage of you. But you've got to organize! There must be thousands of people like you living up here. If you got them all together, you could win!"

"There's a lawyer down in Vancouver named McEachron," Dale said, "won a case like this for a friend of mine. . . ."

"We've got six months before anything happens," Diana said. "My mother knows the District Manager. He's on the school board with her. . . ."

Gilly knew some of the guys down on Quadra. And so they talked.

Yet, all the time I knew they were not going to do it. That it was my style to write letters, to pressure Congressmen, to organize committees—or it used to be, when I was young. Dale wasn't going to form any committee. He was essentially a loner, an artist *manqué* whose life style was his art form. I'd heard him say, as he left the house with Swen, "But you wouldn't want a bunch of summer cottage people up here, would you?"

Diana wasn't going to do it because it wasn't practical, and because, basically, she had no quarrel with the system.

Gilly couldn't have done it even if she wanted to, because she had no sense of herself and, therefore, she could not have a sense of other people, would never be able to draw anyone to her side.

Ellis was all right—Ellis was going to end up being a small businessman in Vancouver. He was a better man than I thought he was at first, but what did Ellis know?

And there was Buddhi, who was *out of it.*

So that left Ben, who was going to build his next house one island north from here, and place it where it would get the morning sun.

I had not unlocked any doors.

Ben had admitted that he did not like being broke or lonely, but his idea of what to do about it still ended, apparently, in being a cooperative of one.

A wise friend of mine once said to me, "The last thing in the world people will give up is their suffering."

Perhaps it would take him another twenty years to learn that there were more than two choices; that the alternative to being a pampered dog was not, necessarily, to become a lone wolf. Perhaps that inner core, that artist's eye, was so fragile, so vulnerable, that he could only deal with it by denying it. "I had to unlearn a whole lot of things I'd learned from you," he said, "in order to live. I had to develop a tough emotional skin, reduce my emotional commitments nearly to zero."

I had not meant to disarm him, hadn't intended to drive him into this vast indifference to escape the crippling effect of my excessive feeling. It was built-in. It couldn't be helped. To the extent that mothers connected children to life, they also became the creators of conscience. They were responsible for the basic social unit: out of one came two. It was an accident of history that my despair had hit Ben when he was old enough to respond to it, but not old enough to cope with it. Maybe I had burdened him with a guilt he would need a lifetime to undo. But I, too, was a historical accident, a vestigial survivor of the disintegrating nuclear family, subject to the traumas of my time and unable to transcend my own particular history.

I had to put it behind me now; to let him go once and for all.

We stayed at Capaswap Lake that night to watch the eclipse. Astri and Jimmy went to bed believing that I would turn up again in their lives, from time to time, like Ben. The others collected down at the wharf to watch the primal drama being enacted in the sky. The Queen of Night rode high above the curving hills. As the shadow of the earth bit into her flank, she flushed, her color deepening from white to orange. Deeper and deeper moved the devouring shadow, violating her wholeness, and deeper she flushed until she was as red as blood.

The shadow grew larger and larger still, until all that remained of her body was a smoldering ruin. She was annihilated, utterly. Yet, at the moment of consummation, the Director turned up the wattage on the stars. On the black satin surface of the lake, the starlight flowed, ecstatic, and the whole cosmos of earth and sky seemed to wheel like a great revolving disc. From the darker hills of the western

rim to the dipping valleys on the east, each separate darkness asserted its own form. No bird called in the night, no
ripple of water broke the silence. And then the silver
thread appeared, growing longer, broader, swelling as the
moon took her life back into herself. I could not leave until
she was delivered, and scarcely noticed when the others
moved off down the path, one by one. I was alone and giddy
with the moon's divinity.

Perhaps Dale returned to the lakeshore because he was
the only one, besides myself, who was old enough to take
an eclipse personally.

"Before you leave," he said very softly, "I wanted to
say thank you—for Ben. He is an amazing person."

"Yes," I said, "he is."

I could not say to Dale "You're welcome," because he
was not. "You mean a great deal to Ben," I said. "You make
his living here possible."

"No," Dale said, "you have it wrong. It is he who
makes my living here possible."

The moment he said it I knew it was not idle talk, that
it was profoundly true. That Ben was the son, the brother,
the friend, the true believer who made Dale's own unbelief
bearable. That Ben filled his hollow space, redeemed him.

"I came here intending to fight you, Dale."

"I know you did."

"But I've laid down my arms. You've won."

"Do you think so?" he said, musing. "I wonder."

The last of the earth's shadow passed beyond the
moon, became a wandering hole in the sky, a moving finger
of darkness—a great nothing of a greater something.
"Would you like me to take you across in the canoe? The
others are walking."

"Yes, I would like that," I said, for I wanted no mundane farewells. Dale found my hand in the darkness and helped me into his canoe. He paddled across the black satin surface like an Indian, without making a sound; as baffling, as invisible a spirit, as unknowable to me now as he'd been before I came.

16

There is a certain wind that springs up when the night rolls over in its sleep, anticipating day. I heard that wind and watched it toss in the tops of the trees above the Kiosk, brushing against the steadfast stars. It was nearly time to go, and I had yet to see Ben's lake by moonlight. I was braver now. Yesterday I'd climbed the mountain with Ben, I'd seen his tree and had a vision, and my heart was filled with gratitude. Stealthy as a cat, I lifted the heavy door of the Kiosk and slipped out into the darkness, down, down the soft slope, bracing my weight against the rough bark of trees lest on this, my last morning, I lose my nerve, and fall.

"Good-bye," I said to the round, bright moon. "Good-bye," I said to the lake, to the mountains, to the great cedar stump beside the water. For I was leaving with the dawn, and Ben was coming with me.

"It's a propitious time for a journey," he'd said as we

left Buddhi's island, returning home. "It will be easy crossing Dyer Strait with three of us paddling the canoe."

Dawn was still an hour away, but the forest was forming, assuming its pillared shape, emerging from dream. I
dressed quickly and hurried down to the little house, winding my watch. Ben was up and stirring, too, unable to wait
for dawn. He had the fire going and sent me to the creek
to fill the water bucket.

He put a batch of biscuits in the Airtight to bake and
opened the last can of ham, cut it into thin slices, some for
now, the rest to keep us on our journey. "Will it take long,
Ben, to go by canoe?"

"We should reach Vancouver Island before noon," he
said, "if we catch the tide at the slack." He and Buddhi had
worked it out with the Tide Book. The tide turned at seven
at Tibbett Bay. It would take about two hours to circle the
south shore of Proctor's Island, half an hour to rest at Camp
Nought; and the final sprint across Dyer Strait—three
miles of steady paddling across open ocean—depended on
the current. "Will we see any whales, do you think?"

"I doubt that we'll be that lucky," he replied.

"And will you go to see this man, McEachron, in Vancouver?"

"Most likely."

"And have you somewhere to stay in the city?"

"Sure. There's this girl I met at art school—the one
who gave me the seeds for my garden? I'll probably meet
Ellis down there, too. See if I can help him sell the shakes."

"And Buddhi?"

"Buddhi's going to a Zen session in Vancouver. Then
he's taking off for California to see his daughter."

"A necessary obeisance to the Mysteries," Buddhi told

me, describing his ecstasy floating about Tibbett Lake in the kayak with the cosmos mirrored in his mind. "To purify me for parenthood."

Ben's larder was nearly empty. Whatever would not keep for several weeks, he tucked into his backpack to take along. Last night we'd used the last of the old onions, but new onions were sprouting in his garden; tiny, tentative shoots among the weeds. The little house was tidy, the dishes washed and stacked behind the Airtight, the soap dish covered, a little pile of kindling on the floor beside the stove, the two new chairs stowed side by side under the workbench. The only evidence of my brief residence was the little stove handle hanging behind the Airtight, and the unnatural cleanliness of the bottom of the dishpan.

Everything was packed and ready. Only my suitcase and sleeping bag remained at the Kiosk. I followed Ben up the hill to fetch them, and, while I stuffed the down-filled nylon into the case, I noticed Ben walking around outside, studying the ground. "Did you drop something?" I asked.

"No," he said, "but I was just noticing . . . there's wolf spoor here. There's a considerable amount of wolf spoor."

The little beach uttered a gravelly cry of farewell as we pushed off in Buddhi's canoe. Save for the moon's reflection, the lake was a spoon of darkness. Darkness veiled Ben's tree and the mountain's mass, but behind Ben's camp the sky was turning pearly.

It was a quarter to six when we reached Buddhi's island, climbed up the path to sit in his ashram while he completed his preparations. It was a low-ceilinged dome draped with Indian scarves, with poster-sized photographs of dark-eyed, wizened, bearded gurus ranged around the walls. He served us fresh coffee in mugs taken from underneath a sleeping platform. While we sipped it, he bashed a number of tin cans with a rock and tucked them underneath a second sleeping platform. Shook the leftover crumbs of his breakfast from an iron skillet, brushed it out with his sleeve before hanging it from a nail. Stuffed the smaller of his two *go* boards into a burlap sack with a bright red label that said MAINE POTATOES.

As we glided past the pterodactyl that guarded Buddhi's harbor, a white sunrise broke over the mountain and a covey of birds rose, like hope, from the lake.

A long portage lay between the lake and Tibbett Bay. When we arrived at Earl and Stukey's inlet, Ben took all the baggage out of the canoe and told me I'd be better off taking Harry Fox's trail, for there would be a good deal of open water to cross now that Earl and Stukey were making up the logs into rafts. "Do you think they might come out shooting if they hear voices?" I whispered to Ben. "Don't be silly," he whispered back. "Then why are you whispering?" I wanted to know.

Ben and Buddhi carried the canoe overhead, while I struggled through the brittle-boughed salal, which tore at my jacket, snapped at my eyes, clawed at my hair. I got caught in thickets, put my foot deep into an animal's burrow, snagged my sleeping bag in the narrow space between trees. "Ouch!" I cried to the vengeful thickets, "I'm going! You don't have to push!"

It took two trips to carry both the canoe and the cargo across the inlet. Stukey and Earl had churned up a lot of mud since we'd been here last, but the logs from Tibbett Lake were all lined up and ready to go. The sea was up, lapping at the rocks and covering the base of the long island in the bay. Anchored in its lee was a white-nosed yacht with an on-shore tent, very Abercrombie and Fitch. Two small children stood at the edge of the island, just where Ben and I had eaten our lunch and watched the spurting clams. They did not respond when I waved. A dog bounded out of the tent and barked, and then a mother came out, collected the children and the dog, and herded them all back inside the tent.

Buddhi filled three plastic containers with fresh water from the western fork of the creek. He and Ben rolled themselves a supply of smokes for the journey. I took out my watch. "Exactly seven o'clock!" I said, and Ben confirmed that the tide was, indeed, turning from high slack to low slack.

"The Tide Book's as close to absolute truth as the *I Ching,*" I said. Ben laughed. "Yup, it times the tide to the minute, but nobody on the island owns a watch!"

Earl and Stukey had enclosed the whole of the harbor with a continuous string of logs, chained together end to end. This boom contained the timber that was to be pulled through the flume, so that it would not drift out to sea before it was made up into rafts. I do not remember Ben or Buddhi discussing their plan for crossing the boom, in advance. We all climbed into the canoe and paddled out as far as the boom, at which point Ben instructed me to get out and stand at the far end of a log while he and Buddhi lifted the laden canoe over a chain. Not one of us fell into the water. Both of them got their feet wet. I, be it here recorded, did not.

It was seven-thirty when we passed the tip of the long island at which Tibbett Bay joined the sea. A whistle blew at the Company camp, and the power saws began to grind, proclaiming the presence of progress in paradise.

Now the sun was wide awake, gleaming on the vast expanse of water on which the canoe was no larger than a thimble. Seaweed floated past, and the waves crossing the strait struck the rocky shore of Proctor's Island resoundingly, breaking up the pattern of gluck! thunk! swonk! under the thin metal bottom of the canoe. We rode the slack tide out, traveling with the current, rounding the island's southern rim. For better than two hours we paddled in perfect unison, talking little, saving our energy for the work. "Will it be like this when we cross open water?" I asked Ben. "Is it very far to the other side?"

"Less than an hour from Proctor's Island to Phoenix, if we don't drift south on the current."

Canoeing from Tibbett Bay to Camp Nought was a comprehensible adventure, for we were never more than fifty yards from land. I did not permit myself to consider whales, or the wakes of turbine-powered freighters. I shut out dream-memories of high, stone cliffs and deep, black whirlpools and allowed myself to be reassured by Buddhi's low-keyed report of crossing the strait in a gale six weeks ago with two hundred pounds of groceries for the cooperative as ballast, and only being blown two miles off course. "We're really lucky today," he said. "No wind to speak of, the water like glass . . ."

It was a great relief to get out of the canoe and rest at Camp Nought. Of course, the shakes were gone from the old float, but a business boat was tied up there now, with a large radar screen on the wheelhouse and no one inside. Ben and Buddhi took off their shoes and socks to dry them in the sun. We drank the fresh water and ate dry biscuits and raisins. Ben waited until Buddhi went off into the bushes before offering me a chew of jerky for quick energy. He was exquisitely respectful of Buddhi's vegetarian sensibilities.

We spent nearly an hour resting, enjoying the sunshine. Ben had friends at Phoenix who would give us a lift out to the highway, from where we'd hitch a ride thirty-five miles south to Campbell River.

"The one thing I'm sorry about is that I didn't get to meet Ray Beame, my most exotic reader," I said. Indeed, had the Fairharbor Lighthouse not been a good ten miles south of Phoenix, I'd have tried to persuade Ben to go there instead. It still looked magical to me, a reference point for all the barges and scows and tugs and freighters and container ships that passed before it and beyond it, taking the inland passage down the east coast of Vancouver Island to the big city.

At eleven o'clock we climbed back into the canoe. We were about to push off when two men in helmets and dark glasses hurried across the pebbly beach and boarded the gray boat, gunned up the motor, and farted out of the harbor.

"Maybe they'll pick us up on the radar screen," Buddhi observed.

I undid my shoelaces in preparation for the grand crossing, just in case. We threaded between a barren rock adorned with strutting gulls and a cliff that rose seventy feet up from the sea, a granite wall without a crack or a fissure. And then we met the southbound current, a torrent within a flood that traveled downhill and met the tide in a series of deep, black whirlpools. I'd seen it in hundreds of nightmares, except that now I was not standing on top of the rock trying to scream while Ben drowned. He and I were in the same boat.

"Give it all you've got!" Ben cried, translating my panic into muscle power. I concentrated on the perfect coordination of my stroke with Buddhi's, with the rippling muscles under his tee shirt, on the cacophony of water beneath the canoe. We shot out of whirlpool range and away from shore, our gunnels a mere three inches above the level of the waves. Under the largest sky, across the broadest sea, we were lighter than a toy and too insignificant for tragedy. For the last time, perhaps, I knew the outrageous luxury of being young.

It was high noon when we entered the harbor, a beach strewn with sea wrack and old rubber tires, with a rotting wharf jutting into the shallows. There was no brass band. No whistles blew, no flags were flying. There was not a single human being in sight. Nor would we find anyone in a short walk to the center of town, because Phoenix was a ghost town, abandoned some ten years ago after the territory was logged out.

"Eleven miles to the highway?" I said, looking down the dusty road that ended at the beach. "Looks like its been months since a car passed this way."

Buddhi sat down to rest beside his burlap bag. "I wouldn't worry," he said, lighting up a smoke. "We've got plenty of karma."

Ben's friends comprised the entire present population of Phoenix. Their house had burned to the ground some six months before and they were housed temporarily in a chicken coop. But they were not at home.

"So what do we do? Walk?"

"Well, before we do anything, let's eat!" said Ben.

We finished the last of the supplies in the backpack and saved only one of the containers of fresh water, in case of emergency. As Ben and Buddhi were finishing off their smokes, a cloud of dust appeared far down the road, grew larger and louder until it became a Ford van which stopped ten feet from where we sat. If Buddhi had rubbed a magic lamp with his sleeve to materialize this wonder, I could not have been more astonished.

The man who climbed out and shook hands with Ben looked like a model from the Sears catalogue: smiling, modest, scrubbed, and pressed. "Long time no see!" he said to Ben. It was Ray Beame, the keeper of the Fairharbor Lighthouse. "I just happened to be passing by," he said when Ben introduced us.

Ray said that Ben's friends, who were also friends of his, had gone down to Campbell River for the day to negotiate a bank loan. Dale had made the phone call, which resulted in the pick-up of the shakes, from the lighthouse, and Ray reported that they had, indeed, gone off on schedule.

"This is who would see the flares!" I realized. For, surely, Ray was the one person in the whole area who kept his eye on things, and a far-reaching eye it was.

"Say," he asked diffidently, "could I give you folks a lift anywhere?"

By the time we were well on our way south to Campbell River, Ray said he'd seen a flash of sunlight on metal out in the strait during the morning, looked through the telescope and seen three people in a canoe. Since Ben and Buddhi were the only two people who could possibly be taking a canoe from Tibbett Bay to Phoenix, he deduced that the person in the middle had to be Ben's mother. So he thought he'd take a fast run up to Phoenix to see if we were interested in a ride into town. "I guess it's the only chance I'll ever have to meet a living author," he said shyly.

"To the Discovery Inn," I said to Ray. "It isn't every day I have the occasion to take three distinguished gentlemen out to dinner."

I rather enjoyed the curious glances that greeted us as we entered BankAmericard Territory. The hatcheck girl received Buddhi's burlap sack from him without comment, and the hostess suffered a long moment of acute uncertainty, unable, I thought, to begin to list the items of haberdashery required to make either Ben or Buddhi admissible to the dining room. Fortunately, Ray Beame looked respectable enough to legitimatize us all.

"A fruit plate," Buddhi said to the waiter. When it was set before him, he exclaimed again and again over its beauty, what a perfect day it had been, how amply the karma was flowing.

Ben and Ray and I stuffed ourselves with heartier fare. Muzak flowed like syrup over the subdued clatter of cutlery. A row of orange lights on a stainless steel counter warmed the dinner plates. Outside the glass doors of the carpeted dining room, tourists disported themselves in a kidney-shaped, heated swimming pool. Ben reported that the water in the porcelain flush toilets was colored blue.

Suddenly I was seized with grief for something lost and irretrievable.

"I'm dying for the island!" I said.

Buddhi threw a teaspoon into the air and cried exultantly, "It worked, Ben! It worked!"

We hitched a ride from Campbell River to Nanaimo, where a three-hour ferry crossed the bay from Vancouver

Island to the mainland of British Columbia. Dyer Strait became Georgia Strait at the southern end of the inland passage. The ferry that crossed it was an ocean-going vessel, large enough to carry several hundred passengers. It felt odd to be among many people, to eat in the ship's cafeteria, to scan the rows of scenic postcards, to read newspaper headlines black with worldly disaster. I left Ben and Buddhi playing a game of *go* in the ship's lounge and went aloft to watch the sunset from an upper deck. I stood in the wind, hugging Ben's promise to my chest. "I'll never spend another winter alone. It's no good. It's like—only seeing out of one eye."

Purple mountains, diamond-studded with Nanaimo's lights, rimmed the bay. What color Ben had given my life! He'd extrapolated my thought, led me into strange territories, taught me some harrowing truths and some holy ones. It was more than many sons did for their mothers.

"Before you leave, I want you to see my tree," Ben had said as we'd paddled back to his campsite from Buddhi's island yesterday.

We'd beached the canoe beside the great stump and took the lakeside path, circling above the tangle of vines that had barred Gilly's way. "I've only taken this path once since my dog . . . died," Ben said as we began a crooked ascent up the side of the mountain.

We came out on a narrow ledge of rock overlooking Tibbett Lake. Distant hills were falling into shadow, and the livid scar of rock over Forsook Lake glowed in the setting sun.

Ben's tree was a bare-trunked giant whose upper limbs extended far over the tops of its neighbors. A single tuft of

living foliage held a ragged eagle's nest. Across its roots lay
a great windfall, barring access to the base of the tree. But
three rough, ax-hewn steps had been gouged out of its
flank. Ben led me up those steps and stood beside the entrance to the tree. It was hollow and huge, its core burned
and blackened by fire. It must have been a shrine, a place
for visions, a spirit place where sacrifices were made to
unknown gods. As my eyes grew accustomed to the darkness, I discerned a figure scratched upon the inner surface
of the wood—the figure of a man falling headlong through
space. I did not know who put it here. It could have been
an Indian sign, or it could have been Ben's own drawing,
his self-portrait.

"No," I thought. "I cannot leave it at that."

There was another truth, and it was just as holy as the
truth inscribed upon the walls. It was a human truth that
had to be asserted in the face of terrible and pitiless gods.

It was not enough to witness the sign. I had to alter it.
I could not be cool, detached, objective. Ben was part of my
life, and what connected us to one another was stronger
than what separated us. We were all fallen angels; our
redemption lay in the lives we shared with one another.

The fingers in my pocket curled around Astri's chalk.
I took it out and drew another falling figure alongside the
first, linking their hands. And then another, and another,
until I covered the blackened walls with a circle of angels,
an ongoing wheel of life.

Ben watched me from the doorway. Far over his head,
a many-hued ring of rainwater formed around the sun. The
eagle's nest was shattered with light.

"It's my message, Ben," I said.

We wept in one another's arms.

"It's time to go now. You've taken very good care of me, Ben . . ."

"Your being here energized everybody—changed everything."

He guided my feet into the footholds hacked out of the great, prone log.

"Do you see these steps?" he said when I reached the rock ledge.

"Yes . . ."

"I cut those steps for you, more than two years ago. I knew, then, that you would come."

FEENIE ZINER directed the Writing Program of the English Department of the University of Connecticut until her retirement. She lives in Branford, Connecticut, with her husband, Zeke Ziner, a printmaker and sculptor. Joe Ziner, the "Ben" of this book, is an artist, printer, and publisher of the Percolator Press of Courtenay, British Columbia.